Small Pleasures

Joyful Recipes *for* Difficult Times

BLOOMSBURY PUBLISHING

LONDON • OXFORD • NEW YORK • NEW DELHI • SYDNEY

Contents

Introduction:

Comfort ✦ 14

Restoration ✦ 70

Pleasure ✦ 128

Pleasure –
a feeling of enjoyment
or satisfaction, or something
that produces this feeling.

Me – From Life Kitchen
to Small Pleasures

Those who know me may be familiar with the journey that led me to where I am today. But, for those who don't, understanding what drives me helps to make sense of everything that is in this book, and to understand the life events that underpin and inspire everything else I do.

My mother died as a result of small cell lung cancer in 2013, when I was just twenty years old. The impacts of this disease, its treatment and the side effects of that treatment on both my mother and us as a family as we supported her compelled me to do something meaningful. After my mother died, I set out to find ways I could improve the awfulness of the effects of living with cancer for others.

There followed hours and hours of late-night conversations and brainstorming and – eventually – I had a light-bulb moment. The answer was Life Kitchen.

Based in northeast England, Life Kitchen is a small family-run organisation that provides cookery classes and tasting experiences for people who live with the side effects of cancer and its treatments – just as my mother had lived with them. Since Life Kitchen's formation in 2018, we have led classes all over the UK, collaborated with charities and organisations that work with people living with cancer and supported hundreds of people who have had their senses altered as a result of the disease or its therapies. Our one, overarching aim is to help people to find pleasure in food again.

Since the release of my first book, *Life Kitchen*, in 2020, the world has changed immeasurably for all of us. On the night of the book's launch event, in central London, the first suggestions of Covid-19 and its potential impact had started to rumble. On the underground, a few commuters were already wearing face masks; for some at the launch, it was the last visit they would make to London – or anywhere – for months, if not years. Covid-19 ushered in a new era of health concerns that ran beyond the immediate effects of the virus – for many, particularly those who caught the earlier strains, there were significant and long-lasting changes to taste and smell, the exact issues I had seen so often result from treatments for cancer. I felt in a position to help and this led to my second book, *Taste & Flavour*, which was a worldwide hit. In its pages, the recipes offered food that focused on bold flavours and textures, and avoided the ingredients (such as garlic) that so many Covid sufferers consistently said had become unpalatable. The recipes were clear, achievable and simple. Not only did they provide a chink of light on how to enjoy food again, I found they also offered a way to keep quietly, mindfully busy through some of the loneliest and darkest days the world had experienced in quite some time.

Thinking back to my personal experience of Covid-19, I am not afraid to say that it took a huge toll on my mental health. Living alone, struggling to find motivation for pretty much anything and falling completely out of love with solo cooking, I had plenty of time for introspection. I began thinking about why I was feeling this way and what I could do to inject some enjoyment back into my daily routine. I wanted to remind myself how therapeutic cooking – and eating – could be. After all, the whole point of Life Kitchen had been to help those who'd lost their love of eating to find it again. I started by returning to easy, reassuring dishes that made me feel comforted or restored, or gave me pleasure to cook and eat. Through these recipes I slowly fell back in love, not just with the process of making the dishes, but also with the idea of looking after myself in a way that suited me perfectly. I began by making small bites that were relatively quick and easy to prepare, and that put little or no pressure on me to break the mould or produce a full-blown meal. All I asked of myself was that each had signature, Life-Kitchen-style bold and exciting flavours. If the plates were small, even incomplete by conventional 'meal' standards, so be it. This was about cooking that was achievable given my state of mind and gave me a moment to feel better.

Realising that I definitely wasn't the only one feeling lost as a result of Covid, I wanted Life Kitchen to provide a way to help, again. We expanded our audience to beyond those living with cancer or suffering the physical after-effects of Covid to those who were suffering mentally, too. We worked closely with the co-director of London's Centre of the Study of the Senses, Professor Barry Smith, just as we had done when we first conceived Life Kitchen, to ensure our work was scientifically robust. With his expertise as our guide, we set about creating a series of recipes that were accessible to follow (easy on the mind), full of flavour (bliss for the senses) and inexpensive to produce (light on the pocket, which has been particularly important during the financial crisis that many families have experienced in recent years).

And this brings us to *Small Pleasures*. With its emphasis on finding (or re-finding) the joy in cooking and eating, this book is, in some ways, less a sequel to *Taste & Flavour* and more the natural follow-up book to the original *Life Kitchen*. This new cook book is the evolution of everything I've learned since 2018 about flavour, people, living with illness and so much more. It brings together all my experiences and understanding, through all the journeys I've had the privilege of sharing with those who are going through hard times. It collects the wisdom of our accumulated Life Kitchen practices in the hope of bringing some enjoyment back into the life of anyone who is struggling – physically, mentally or emotionally.

Throughout the writing process, my focus has been to develop exciting, easy-to-create dishes for when we feel run down, lethargic or blue. Each recipe uses only a few ingredients and is packed with time-efficient hacks and little wins to ensure minimal preparation for maximum deliciousness. Throughout, I have stuck to the key Life Kitchen principle of maximising flavour, while also keeping in mind a commitment to ingredients that are both easy to find and prepare and have well-documented health benefits, particularly for the gut, which I believe is the bedrock of our physical well-being. The aim has been to provide an holistic approach in the recipes: these are dishes packed with bold flavours and good-for-you ingredients that look beautiful on the plate. Together, they create a manifesto for feeling good again; whether you're recovering from illness, running on empty, or feeling low, each recipe is here to nourish and heal, to restore body, mind and soul, and should you need it, to revive your love of cooking and eating.

The Small Pleasures Philosophy

The book is divided into three chapters: Comfort, Restoration and Pleasure. I selected these because they are the three stages of recovery that bring me through the tough times and back to my true self. Each chapter leads into the next to take you on a journey – I like to think of it as an active meditation – that encourages you to focus on gathering a few simple ingredients, to eat and to look after yourself, when eating and looking after yourself may seem your lowest priorities. Most of the recipes make one or two servings, because they are meant just for you (or to eat one and store one), as a treat – a small pleasure for your day. (Of course, if you want to share them, that's wonderful, too.)

This isn't a wellness book. It doesn't give you the tools to overcome stress, or realign your life so that you stop skipping meals to cram in a few extra hours of work. It doesn't even make claim to boost your immunity or restore your nutritional balance. Rather, this book is about the power of taste and flavour – a moment of joy from a morsel of deliciousness that hits the senses and provides a brief distraction to lift the spirit in a way that lingers far longer in the memory than the meal itself. I want these simple recipes to show you that pleasure in food doesn't have to be complicated – and it's available to all of us, time and again, whatever our mood or level of physical well-being.

Comfort

This chapter is for when you feel at your worst, when eating is a chore, but you know that a plate or bowl of something familiar and reassuring will bring you solace. With that in mind, these recipes are classics with a twist – think pastas, eggs, stews and potatoes – all with flavour and simplicity woven into their core. These dishes are my edible comfort; the first steps in my road map to finding my way back to myself.

Restoration

The recipes in this chapter are designed to reawaken your energy. Their flavours are fresh and tangy, from ingredients intended to enliven the senses and bring a little brightness to life. The added zing in a French Pickled Onion Soup – a tart twist on a well-loved classic – is a particular favourite.

Pleasure

The final chapter is all about indulgence. These flavour-packed recipes are easy wins with clever flavour twists. They are a love letter to yourself; they tell you that you're special as you ready yourself to return to the world.

Key Ingredients

The following eight ingredients are the staples I use time and again throughout the book. They are the ingredients you need always in your store cupboard or fridge, the ones on repeat order for your online shop. Each one of them is incredibly versatile and gives your food a little flavour boost when you really need it. For most of them, a little goes a long way.

Rose harissa paste
This aromatic North African spice blend is predominately made from chilli peppers, paprika and olive oil. It has a strong, heady taste that adds both heat and depth.

Miso
A Japanese paste made from fermented soya beans and rice or barley malt, miso has a salty flavour that brings a certain 'meaty' depth to a dish. Packed with umami (savouriness), miso acts as the key that unlocks the other flavours in the recipes.

Wine vinegar
Acidity is a core building block of flavour, and a few drops of vinegar can transform the way we experience our food. Made by fermenting white or red wine, this condiment brings the sourness you would expect of a vinegar, but with a light and slightly fruity tang. Red wine vinegar has a slightly more savoury flavour than white wine vinegar, which tends to be marginally lighter in its impact on a dish.

Soy sauce
An Asian condiment made from fermented soya beans, soy sauce has a deep salty flavour and is a rich source of umami. It comes in light and dark forms, which are respectively milder and stronger in flavour, appropriate to the recipe.

Sumac
This Mediterranean and Middle Eastern spice blend is made from the dried berries of the sumac plant. It has a deep red colour and a distinctive citrus tang that lifts and enhances dishes in a way similar to effects of lemon juice or zest.

Za'atar
A Middle Eastern spice blend that often contains a mixture of dried herbs such as sumac, thyme, salt and sesame, za'atar is sharp and aromatic, and deeply savoury.

Maple syrup
Made by part-boiling the sap of certain maple trees, maple syrup gives dishes the sweetness of honey, with an added a hint of vanilla or caramel.

Vanilla paste
Thick and sweet, vanilla paste is made by combining the ground pods and seeds of the vanilla plant. It brings a familiar, smooth flavour and is slightly more intense than vanilla extract (and infinitely better than vanilla essence, which tends to be a processed flavouring). The main difference between the two, though, is that the paste contains the seeds, which will fleck your dishes with their colour and sweetness.

Comfort

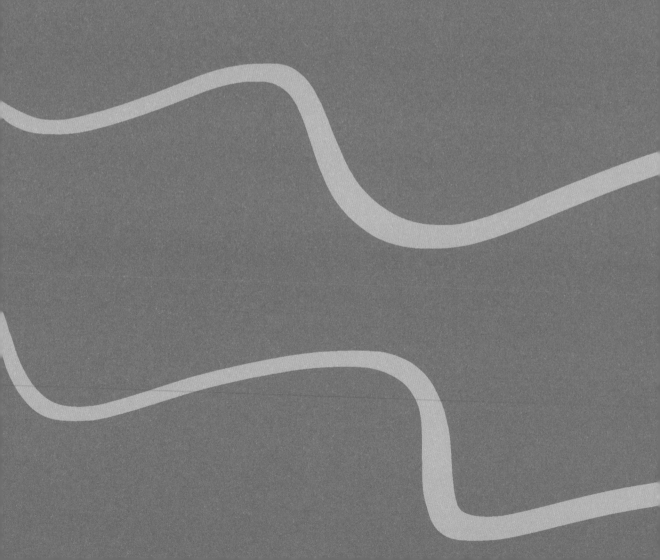

Comfort brings you the familiar, classic dishes of childhood – each with a Life Kitchen spin that ramps up the flavour and, of course, the joy.

Parmesan orzotto with lemon porcini

Orzotto is my simple take on a risotto – simple in that it needs no incessant stirring (thanks to the orzo pasta, rather than rice) and that the straightforward combination of umami-rich porcini mushrooms and parmesan add unparalleled savouriness. The lemony lift is an easy win.

Serves 1

100g orzo
1 vegetable jelly stock pot
25g dried porcini mushrooms, rehydrated in 500ml boiling water, then drained (reserve the soaking liquid)
80g parmesan, grated, plus extra to serve
50g unsalted butter
2 tablespoons olive oil
1 lemon, zest and juice
½ handful of flat-leaf parsley, chopped

Bring a saucepan of well-salted water to the boil. Add the orzo and cook it according to the packet instructions, until al dente.

While the pasta is cooking, melt the stock pot in a large frying pan over a medium heat. Add the soaking liquid from the porcini mushrooms, increase the heat to high and cook until the liquid has reduced by half and thickened (about 5–6 minutes). Add half the parmesan into the frying pan, stirring continuously until combined, then add the rest of the parmesan and stir again.

Scoop and reserve a mugful from the pasta cooking water and then drain the orzo. Add the pasta to the parmesan sauce and stir well to coat. Add the butter, stirring until it has melted and the sauce is combined and glossy, and coats the pasta. Set aside.

Heat the olive oil in a separate frying pan over a medium–high heat. When hot, add the rehydrated mushrooms and fry them for 6 minutes, until they are crisp. Remove the frying pan from the heat and add the lemon juice to the pan, letting it sizzle and flavour the porcini.

To finish the orzotto, stir the lemon zest and parsley through the pasta. Spoon it into a bowl and serve it topped with the crispy, lemony mushrooms and sprinkled with extra parmesan.

Miso scrambled eggs with spring onions

Soft and unctuous scrambled eggs are pretty perfect just as they are, but adding miso paste elevates them from a hard-to-fault classic to a rich and luxurious treat. A final flourish of vibrant spring onions, which bring tang, and a sprinkling of nigella seeds for texture make this much-loved comforter truly exceptional.

Serves 1

50g unsalted butter, sliced
2 eggs
1½ teaspoons white miso
salt and ground black pepper

To serve
1 slice of warm, toasted
   sourdough bread
a sprinkling of nigella seeds
1 spring onion, finely sliced

Add the butter slices to a cold, medium frying pan. Crack two eggs into the pan and gently break up the yolks with a wooden spoon. Turn the heat on to low, and cook, stirring continuously, until the butter melts and combines with the eggs. Continue stirring while the eggs start to come together and the mixture begins to thicken.

At this point, add the miso and stir well, ensuring it is evenly incorporated.

Season the scramble with salt and pepper to taste and immediately spoon it over your warm, toasted sourdough. Scatter over the nigella seeds and spring onions to serve.

Brie, cheddar and harissa toastie

Ginger paste might seem an unlikely addition to a toastie, but it adds a fiery balance that elevates this combination of cheeses and spice to princely status. It's a simple trick that knocks the socks off toasties as you know them.

Serves 1

75g brie
100g extra-mature cheddar,
  grated
1 teaspoon rose harissa paste
2 slices of white bread
1 teaspoon ginger paste
a small knob of unsalted butter
  and a splash of vegetable oil,
  for frying

Pop the brie in a bowl and use a fork to soften it. Add the majority of the cheddar (reserve just enough for a layer of sprinkled cheese) and mash the two cheeses together, then add the harissa paste, mixing until evenly combined.

Spread one side of each slice of bread thinly with ginger paste. On one slice cover the paste with the cheese mixture, then sprinkle the reserved grated cheddar on top. Place the other slice of bread on top, ginger paste downwards, to create a sandwich.

Melt the butter with the splash of oil in a medium frying pan over a medium heat. Carefully transfer your sandwich into the pan and toast it for 5 minutes on each side, until golden brown on the outside with an oozy, melty middle. Remove the toastie to a plate, slice it in half, and serve.

Thai basil and coconut chicken stew

Umami really comes to out to play in this quick but rich stew, with coconut milk, tomatoes, and soy and fish sauces all providing savoury synergy. Thai basil is a favourite of mine and here it brings vibrancy, while the spices add a darting lift. This is a 30-minute midweek meal that doesn't hold back when it comes to warming, satisfying flavour explosion.

Serves 2

6 boneless chicken thighs, cut into bite-sized pieces
4 tablespoons garlic paste
4 tablespoons ginger paste
1 teaspoon ground coriander
¼ teaspoon white pepper, plus extra to season
½ teaspoon salt, plus extra to season
1 tablespoon vegetable oil
3 long red (Thai) chillies, finely chopped with seeds (keep back a few slices to garnish)
100g Thai basil leaves, finely chopped, plus extra to garnish
1 × 400g tin of full-fat coconut milk
300ml chicken stock
10 mixed-colour cherry tomatoes, halved
1 teaspoon fish sauce
1 teaspoon light soy sauce
1 teaspoon light brown soft sugar
steamed vegetables and boiled jasmine rice, to serve

Place the diced chicken into a bowl and add the garlic, ginger, ground coriander, white pepper and salt and mix well. Leave to marinate overnight if you have time, but for at least 10 minutes.

When you're ready to cook, heat the oil in a large saucepan over a medium–high heat. Add in the marinated chicken and fry it for 5–6 minutes, turning, until the chicken begins to brown. Add the chillies and half of the basil, followed by the coconut milk and chicken stock. Simmer for 15 minutes, then add the cherry tomatoes, fish sauce, soy sauce and sugar, and simmer for a further 5 minutes, until the tomatoes are just softened and the chicken is cooked through. Remove the stew from the heat, season with salt and extra white pepper, and stir through the remainder of the basil. Scatter over the extra basil leaves and the chilli slices to garnish.

Serve with steamed vegetables and cooked jasmine rice.

Black garlic, tomato and cheese open sandwich

A classic pairing of cheese and tomato provides the familiarity in this sandwich, while adding black garlic gives it the flavour lift. I leave the sandwich 'open', on flat breads, as I think it's the best way to admire its beauty.

Serves 1

2 black garlic cloves, grated
75g extra-mature cheddar, grated
1 spring onion, finely chopped
1 teaspoon white miso
1 tablespoon mayonnaise
2 small flat breads
1 heritage tomato, halved
  and sliced
6 mixed, pitted olives, halved
12 small basil leaves
salt and ground black pepper

In a medium bowl, mix together the garlic, cheddar, spring onion, miso and mayo until combined.

Divide the mixture equally between the flat breads and spread it out into an even layer. Top each flat bread with the tomato slices, olive halves and basil leaves. Season with salt and pepper, then serve.

6-ingredient miso tomato sauce

Rarely have six ingredients been such good friends. Miso provides a salty, umami richness to an already savoury sauce, which – given that everything is roasted together – is super-simple to make. It is perfect for pasta, vegetables or roast chicken.

Serves 2

500g mixed-colour cherry
   tomatoes
2 teaspoons white miso
90ml olive oil
1 × 400g tin of chopped
   tomatoes
2 tablespoons red wine vinegar
½ handful of basil, shredded
salt and ground black pepper

Preheat the oven to 200°C/180°C fan.

In a baking dish, toss together the cherry tomatoes with the miso and oil, until coated, then season with salt. Add the chopped tomatoes, give everything a stir and place the baking dish in the oven. Cook the tomato-y mixture until the cherry tomatoes are collapsed and charred (about 1 hour). Remove the dish from the oven and stir through the vinegar and basil. Return the sauce to the oven for 15 minutes, until all the flavours have combined. Season to taste with salt and pepper.

Serve over pasta, vegetables or roast chicken.

Prawn aglio e olio orzo

The classic Italian dish of aglio e olio (garlic and oil) is almost unbeatable, but bringing prawns to the party adds meatiness, and using orzo (rather than the more usual spaghetti or linguine) provides a wonderfully chewy texture. All in all, the humble original quickly becomes a warm hug in a bowl.

Serves 1

75g orzo
3 tablespoons olive oil
6 raw prawns (defrosted if frozen)
2 garlic cloves, sliced
1 teaspoon chilli paste
2 flat-leaf parsley sprigs, leaves
  picked and finely chopped
1 teaspoon chilli flakes

Bring a saucepan of well-salted water to the boil. Add the orzo and cook it according to packet instructions, until al dente.

Meanwhile, warm the oil in a small frying pan over a medium heat. Add the prawns and cook until pink (about 2–3 minutes), then add the sliced garlic, and cook for 1–2 minutes, until it is very lightly browned (don't let it burn). Immediately stir through the chilli paste and keep the sauce warm until the orzo is ready.

Drain the orzo and add it to the oil and garlic mixture. Sprinkle in the parsley and finish with a scattering of chilli flakes.

Chilli, pea and parmesan dip

Peas, chilli and parmesan are classics together, blitzed into a stunning dip.

Serves 1

100g frozen peas, defrosted
1 tablespoon chilli oil
50g parmesan, finely grated
1 lemon, zest and juice
2 tablespoons olive oil
your favourite crudités and
  crackers, to serve

Put the peas, chilli oil, parmesan, lemon zest and juice and olive oil in a small food processor and blitz them together until smooth and fully combined.

Transfer the dip to a bowl and serve it with crudités and crackers.

Roasted courgette
with lemon, kefir and mascarpone

Kefir is a probiotic yoghurt drink that brings so much goodness to the gut. Here, I've used it with courgette, lemon and mascarpone for a spring/summer vibe, but, in truth, realistically it is a light lunch or side that is delicious all year round.

Serves 1

1 courgette, quartered
   lengthways
2 tablespoons olive oil
2 teaspoons rose harissa paste
juice of 1 lemon
75ml kefir
2 tablespoons mascarpone
½ teaspoon sea salt
big pinch of ground white
   pepper

Heat the oven to 200°C/180°C fan.

Using a sharp knife, score a criss-cross pattern all down the cut sides of the courgette quarters, and place them, cut sides upwards, in a roasting tin.

In a bowl, mix together the olive oil and the rose harissa until combined and brush the mixture all over the courgettes.

Transfer the tin to the oven and roast the courgettes for 12 minutes, until tender and caramelised.

Meanwhile, reserve a little of the lemon juice to sprinkle over at the end, then, in a separate bowl, whisk together the remaining juice and all the remaining ingredients except the pepper. Set aside.

Once the courgettes are cooked, create a bed of the kefir mixture on a plate and top with the roasted courgettes. Finish by sprinkling over the white pepper and the reserved lemon juice.

Marmite cheddar jackets

My mother's cheesy jacket potatoes were a staple of my childhood, so for me there is little that could be more comforting. Adding Marmite and spring onions transforms them into baked dark deliciousness.

Serves 1

1 baking potato
100g extra-mature cheddar,
  grated
1 tablespoon Marmite
1 tablespoon unsalted butter
1 spring onion, finely chopped
a few flat-leaf parsley sprigs,
  leaves picked and chopped,
  to serve

Preheat the oven to 200°C/180°C fan.

Pop the potato on a baking tray on the top rack of the oven and bake it for 45–60 minutes, or until crisp on the outside and soft on the inside. Remove the potato from the oven, but leave the oven on.

Cut the cooked potato in half and scoop out the soft flesh into a bowl. Add the remaining ingredients to the bowl, mix well, and spoon the filling back into the potato skins. Return the potato halves to the baking tray, open sides upwards, and bake for a further 10 minutes, until the tops are golden and crispy. Sprinkle with parsley, to serve.

Harissa baked camembert

Harissa adds heat and fragrant spice to the gooey pungency of the camembert in this recipe. Sweetness comes from the honey and herbiness from the thyme. The results are so moreish you'll be grateful and relieved at how quick the dish is to pull together.

Serves 2

2 tablespoons rose harissa paste
2 tablespoons runny honey
5 thyme sprigs, leaves picked
  and finely chopped, plus extra
  leaves to garnish
1 whole camembert
savoury crackers, crusty bread
  or a few cooked veg, to serve

Preheat the oven to 180°C/160°C fan.

In a bowl mix together the harissa, honey and chopped thyme leaves until the mixture has the consistency of a loose paste. Place the camembert into an ovenproof dish just bigger than the round itself and slather the paste over the top of the cheese. Bake the camembert for 30 minutes, until golden, oozing and bubbling. Serve with crackers, bread or cooked veg for dunking.

Smashed and curried leftover potatoes and peas

Potato and peas sound like an unlikely combination for an umami-rich dish, but this recipe finds its stride with spices and the sharp hit of vinegar, giving not only comforting, mouthwatering depth, but sweet acidity, too. The aim is to use leftover new potatoes, for the ultimate re-style, but, of course, you can cook the potatoes from scratch instead, if you need.

Serves 1

1 teaspoon curry powder
1 teaspoon garam masala
3 tablespoons olive oil
1 green chilli, finely chopped
  with seeds
6 leftover cooked new potatoes,
  smashed down with a spatula
100g frozen peas, thawed
2 tablespoons red wine vinegar
a few spoonfuls of full-fat extra-
  thick Greek yoghurt mixed with
  chopped coriander or another
  favourite herb, to serve

Preheat the grill to its highest setting.

In a bowl mix together the curry powder, garam masala, olive oil and chopped green chilli. Reserve a little bit of the spice mixture for the peas and use the remainder to coat the potatoes. Spread out the flavoured potatoes over a baking tray and pop them under the grill for 8–10 minutes, turning occasionally, until they are crisp.

Meanwhile, coat the peas in the reserved spice mixture, then add them to the baking tray with the potatoes during the final minute of the potato cooking time, until warmed through. Remove the vegetables from the grill, drizzle with the vinegar and serve with the herby yoghurt.

Sweetcorn and harissa spring onion mash

Is there any food more comforting than perfect mashed potato? It feels almost a sin to add new ingredients to this well-loved side dish, but I couldn't argue with the addition of North African harissa paste balanced with the sweet hit of sweetcorn kernels.

Serves 2

2 large potatoes, peeled and
  quartered
1 × 200g tin of sweetcorn in
  water, drained
2 tablespoons rose harissa paste
2 tablespoons unsalted butter
2 spring onions, chopped

Bring a small saucepan of salted water to the boil over a medium heat. Add the potatoes and cook for about 16–18 minutes, or until fork tender.

Drain the potatoes and add them back to the pan. Place the pan over a medium heat, then add the sweetcorn and mash it all together with a potato masher until combined and smooth. Add the harissa and butter and stir until combined. Finally, fold through the spring onions to evenly distribute, spoon into bowls and serve.

Ultimate mushrooms on toast

Mushrooms, fire and a good slab of toasted bread, this familiar dish is introduced to other culinary heroes, such as smoked hummus, to form a new staple for your repertoire. The umami-rich mushrooms take centre stage when paired with the aniseed-y tarragon, salty miso and zingy lemon.

Serves 1

1 tablespoon olive oil
100g mixed mushrooms, sliced
  or quartered
1 lemon, zest and juice
1 teaspoon white miso
3 tarragon sprigs, leaves picked
  and chopped
1 slice of sourdough bread
1 tablespoon smoked hummus

Heat the oil in a medium frying pan over a high heat. Add the mushrooms and lemon zest and fry for 5–7 minutes, until the mushrooms are deeply golden. Add the miso, lemon juice and tarragon, then stir to coat the mushrooms. Fry the mushrooms for a further 2–3 minutes, until they are dark and delicious. Remove the pan from the heat and set aside.

While the mushrooms are finishing off, toast your sourdough to your liking.

Spread the hummus over the toast and top it with the mushroom mixture to serve.

Cheese and sesame egg crumpet

It's almost impossible to imagine anything more comforting than a warm crumpet slathered in butter – but add cheese and an egg and a whole new level of feel-good sumptuousness awaits. My sesame egg is the King of Eggs, adding a nutty undertone and some crunch to the whole treat.

Serves 1

1 sourdough crumpet
1 teaspoon green pesto
50g brie, thinly sliced
1 tablespoon olive oil
1 egg
1 teaspoon sesame seeds, toasted

Preheat your grill to medium.

Toast the crumpet to your liking and spread the pesto evenly over the top. Add the sliced brie and pop the crumpet under the grill for 3–5 minutes, until the cheese is golden and bubbly.

Meanwhile, heat the oil in a small frying pan over a medium heat. Crack in the egg, frying for about 2 minutes, until the white is just set and the yolk is still runny. Remove the pan from the heat.

Pop your crumpet on a plate, place the egg on top and sprinkle the toasted sesame seeds over to finish.

Black olive, feta and honey twists

This is a contemporary twist on familiar cheese straws. Trigeminal-stimulating mint tempers the saltiness of olives and feta, and the yoghurt lends a creaminess to the finished twists. These are surprising and different in every bite.

Makes 8

100g black olive tapenade
200g feta, crumbled
2 tablespoons mint sauce
1 tablespoon runny honey
2 tablespoons full-fat extra-thick
 Greek yoghurt, plus extra mixed
 with a little runny honey and
 lemon thyme leaves, then
 chilled to serve
2 × 320g sheets of ready-rolled
 puff pastry
1 tablespoon ground black
 pepper

Preheat the oven to 200°C/180°C fan and line two baking trays with baking paper (or the sheet from the ready-rolled pastry, if you like).

In a mixing bowl, combine the tapenade, feta, mint sauce, honey and yoghurt until well combined.

Lay out one of the puff pastry sheets and spread the mixture evenly over the top making sure the sheet is completely covered. Then, place the second sheet directly over, covering the mixture. Transfer the sandwiched pastry on to one of the lined baking trays and put it into the fridge for 20 minutes to firm up.

Remove the baking tray from the fridge, then cut the sandwiched pastry lengthways into 8 equal strips. This is easiest if you use a knife to halve the sheets down the middle, then halve and halve again.

One at a time, take the strips and hold them at either end, gently twisting them 3 times. Place each twisted strip on to the other lined baking tray and sprinkle over the black pepper.

Place the strips into the oven and bake for 25–30 minutes, until golden and crispy. Serve with chilled, flavoured Greek yoghurt for dipping.

Flat bread with miso, pancetta and onion crème fraîche

This is my take on the classic French tarte flambée. I've added miso to the finely sliced onions and crème fraîche, resulting in a luxuriously deep base with a touch of sweetness from the roasted onions.

Serves 1–2

1 onion, finely sliced into half
   moons
1 teaspoon white miso
3 tablespoons crème fraîche
100g cubed pancetta
100g gruyère, grated
400g pre-rolled pizza dough
10 flat-leaf parsley sprigs, leaves
   picked and finely chopped

Preheat the oven to 200°C/180°C fan and line a baking tray with baking paper.

Mix together the sliced onion, miso, crème fraîche, pancetta and gruyère until you have a paste flecked with onion and pancetta.

Lay out the pizza dough on the baking tray, spoon over the mixture and spread it out evenly, leaving a 2.5cm border around the edge. Bake the flat bread in the oven until the top is golden, the pancetta is crispy and the dough is cooked through (about 20 minutes). Sprinkle with the chopped parsley and serve in slices.

Fish-finger sandwich
with pickled onion mayo

Comfort food without fish fingers is like bread without butter. Frozen fish fingers are a must for this recipe – none of those fancy offerings belong here. The trick is adding the sharp tang of pickled onions to the velvety mayonnaise, giving a mound of new-look tartare sauce that requires very little effort to rustle up.

Serves 1

2 or 3 fish fingers
3 pickled onions, finely chopped
2 tablespoons mayonnaise
2 coriander sprigs, finely
  chopped
2 slices of white bread
a little watercress
a few pink pickled onions
  (optional), drained, to taste

Cook the fish fingers according to the packet instructions, until golden and crispy.

Meanwhile, in a bowl mix together the chopped pickled onions, the mayo and the coriander until combined. Set aside until the fish fingers are ready.

Spread half the mayo on to one slice of the bread, top with the cooked fish fingers, the watercress, and the pink pickled onions (if using). Spread the remaining mayo on to the other slice of bread and place it, mayo downwards, on top of the fish fingers. Cut in half to serve.

Green herbs and 'nduja frittata

'Nduja is a unique ingredient from the Calabria region of Italy. Its fiery heat and deliciously herby pork flavour add intensity to a humble frittata. The variety of herbs in this recipe makes sure the results are both fresh and powerful.

*Serves 2 as a snack
or 4 as a side*

3 eggs
10 flat-leaf parsley sprigs, finely
   chopped
10 coriander sprigs, finely
   chopped
10 basil leaves, finely chopped
2 rosemary sprigs, leaves picked
2 thyme sprigs, leaves picked
2 tablespoons 'nduja paste
100ml whole milk

Preheat the grill to its highest setting.

Break the eggs into a bowl and whisk them together with all the herbs and the 'nduja. Gradually incorporate the milk, whisking all the time, until everything is combined.

Place a small, ovenproof non-stick frying pan over medium heat. Add in the egg mixture, leaving it to flow to the edges and settle. Cook for 8–10 minutes, until it's nearly set. Then, transfer the pan to the grill for a few minutes to set the top firm. Remove the frittata from the grill, allow it to stand for a few minutes, then use a spatula to cut it into wedges to serve.

Easy umami noodles

So many of my recipes are umami flavour bombs, but this simple noodle dish comes out on top – not only for its deep intensity but also for just how easy it is to cook. Most of these ingredients are likely already in your store cupboard. Feel free to adjust them to suit your taste.

Serves 2

2 nests of dried egg noodles
1 teaspoon vegetable oil
1 tablespoon garlic paste
1 tablespoon ginger paste
1 tablespoon light soy sauce
1 tablespoon maple syrup
½ tablespoon sesame oil
1 tablespoon chilli oil or
   1 teaspoon dried chilli flakes
½ teaspoon Maggi seasoning

To serve
2 eggs
2 spring onions, finely sliced
nigella seeds, for sprinkling

Bring a pan of water to the boil and drop in the noodles. Cook them for 4 minutes, or according to the packet instructions, until tender. Using tongs or a pasta spoon, remove the noodles to a bowl and set aside. Add the eggs to serve to the boiling water, and cook them for 6 minutes until they are hard boiled, but retain some gooeyness in the yolk. Use the tongs or spoon to remove them from the water and place them into a bowl of cold water to stop them cooking further.

While the eggs are cooking, start the sauce. Heat the oil in a large frying pan over a medium heat. Add the garlic and ginger pastes and fry for 1–2 minutes, until the garlic paste begins to brown. Then, add the soy sauce, maple syrup and sesame oil. Add the cooked noodles, the chilli oil or flakes and the Maggi seasoning and stir well to coat the noodles, leaving everything to heat through for a minute or two while you peel the eggs and slice them in half lengthways.

Divide the noodles between two bowls, top each serving with two egg halves and scatter over the spring onions. Finish each bowl with a sprinkling of nigella seeds.

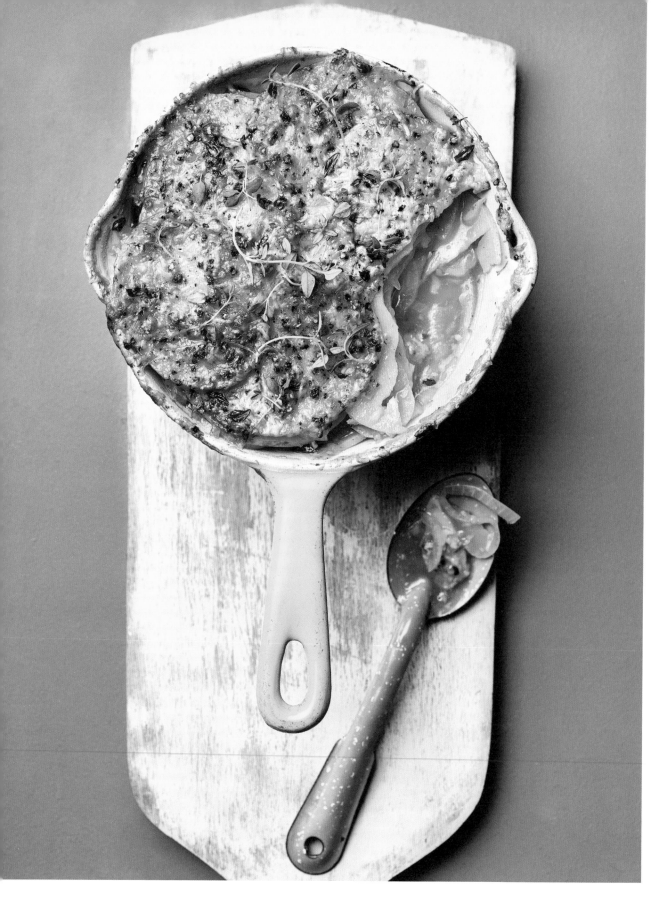

Cheesy potatoes boulangère

Is there any classic that can't be improved with cheese? This take on the French dish is so simple to make that it hardly needs any attention at all. Adding parmesan towards the end of cooking gives a crunchy, tart cheese layer that you have to break through to reach the potato rewards below.

Serves 1

2 potatoes, finely sliced
2 onions, sliced into half moons
2 thyme sprigs, leaves picked,
　plus a few extra sprigs to
　garnish
200ml vegetable stock
75g parmesan, finely grated
salt and ground black pepper

Preheat the oven to 200°C/180°C fan.

In a small baking dish, mix together the potatoes, onions and thyme, season them with salt and pepper, and cover with the vegetable stock.

Place the dish into the oven and bake the potatoes for 45 minutes, then remove and sprinkle over the parmesan. Return the dish to the oven for a final 15 minutes, until the top is golden and the potatoes are tender and piping hot throughout. Garnish with extra thyme sprigs to serve.

Miso and mustard potato salad

Mustard is a simple way to give life to the easiest of dishes. Here, mustard and miso in the dressing turn this into a standout salad worthy of becoming a meal in itself. You have my permission to dig in from the bowl when no one's looking.

Serves 2

For the dressing
2 teaspoons white miso
2 teaspoons maple syrup
2 teaspoons English mustard
2 teaspoons full-fat Greek or
  natural yoghurt
2 teaspoons mayonnaise

For the salad
150g new potatoes, halved
  if large
1 corn on the cob
1 head of baby gem, leaves
  separated and torn
salt and ground black pepper

To serve
1 tablespoon crispy onions
1 teaspoon sumac

Mix together all the dressing ingredients in a large bowl to combine.

Place the new potatoes in a pan of lightly salted, boiling water and cook for about 10–15 minutes, or until tender to the point of a knife. Drain in a colander and leave to steam dry, and cool until warm.

Meanwhile, place a medium, dry frying pan on high heat. Add the corn to the pan and turn it frequently for about 4–5 minutes, until charred all over and the kernels are tender. Remove the pan from the heat and set aside the corn to a plate to cool slightly. Once it is cool enough to handle, hold the cob upright on your work surface and carefully use a sharp knife to slice downwards and strip the kernels from the core. Discard the core.

Tip the warm new potatoes, then the stripped kernels, then the baby gem leaves into the bowl with the dressing. Toss the salad ingredients in the dressing to coat, then season to taste with salt and pepper. Sprinkle the salad with the crispy onions and sumac, and serve.

Sweet-and-sour apple crumble with sweet basil cream

Tamarind isn't something you'd usually find in an apple crumble, but then neither are you likely to find fennel seeds in a crunchy crumble topping. I can assure you, though, that these simple twists do nothing but wow. Sweet-and-sour apple crumble is about to usher you in to a whole new era of dessert deliciousness.

Serves 2

2 eating apples, peeled, cored
   and chopped into 1cm pieces
2 teaspoons tamarind paste
1 teaspoon ground cardamom
1 teaspoon vanilla paste
1 teaspoon caster sugar

For the topping
2 tablespoons caster sugar
45g plain flour
1 teaspoon ground fennel seeds
30g unsalted butter, chilled
   and chopped
1 lemon, zested, to decorate

For the sweet basil cream
10 basil leaves
2 tablespoons golden
   caster sugar
100ml double cream

Preheat the oven to 180°C/160°C fan.

Place the apples, tamarind, cardamom, vanilla, sugar and a splash of water in a small saucepan over a medium heat. Cook for 4–6 minutes, until the apples are soft.

To make the topping, in a bowl, work the sugar, flour, ground fennel and chilled butter together with your fingertips, rubbing until the mixture resembles rough breadcrumbs.

Put the apple mixture into a medium-sized ovenproof dish (about 20–25cm diameter), top it with the crumble mixture in an even layer and bake for 20–25 minutes, or until the top has turned golden brown and the filling is bubbling.

Meanwhile, make the sweet basil cream. Make a basil sugar by pulsing the basil leaves and sugar in a food processor until just combined. Set this aside while you whip the cream to soft peaks. Then, gently fold 1 tablespoon of the basil sugar through the cream until evenly combined. (You can store the remaining basil sugar for another dish; it will keep for up to 3 days in an airtight container, although it may lose some of its vibrant colour – but not its flavour – in that time.)

Scatter the lemon zest over the warm crumble, then serve in spoonfuls with sweet basil cream on the side.

Cinnamon, cardamom and white pepper rice pudding

Rice pudding is the food of my childhood, and I'm not sure there is a dessert I find more comforting. My assistant Rachel kindly brought me her family recipe, which uses bay leaves and white pepper, and it inspired me to find a new take on a premium classic. This version requires very little effort for maximum indulgence.

Serves 2

100g pudding rice
a small knob of unsalted butter,
  to grease the dish
50g caster sugar
350ml whole milk
350ml double cream
1 teaspoon ground cardamom
1 teaspoon ground cinnamon
½ teaspoon ground white pepper
1 teaspoon vanilla extract
1 lemon, zest and juice
1 orange, zest and juice
3 bay leaves

Preheat the oven to 150°C/130°C fan.

Wash and drain the rice until the water runs clear, then butter a medium baking dish (about 20–25cm diameter) thoroughly all over the inside.

In a bowl, mix the rice with all the remaining ingredients apart from the bay leaves. Transfer it to the baking dish, spreading it out evenly, then lay the bay leaves on top. Place the pudding in the oven for about 2 hours, until the rice is tender and the top is golden brown and bubbling. Leave the pudding to stand for 15 minutes, then serve.

Raspberry, blackberry and blueberry baked oats

Berries and lemon are already such a classic combination but when given the warming deliciousness of allspice and cinnamon in a bowl of custard-wrapped oats, they take on a wonderfully new dimension that provides comfort food for the soul.

Serves 2

200g porridge oats
1 teaspoon ground cinnamon
1 teaspoon allspice
3 tablespoons golden
   caster sugar
1 tablespoon white miso
500ml vanilla custard
200ml whole milk
10 raspberries
10 blackberries
10 blueberries
zest and juice of 1 lemon
1 teaspoon demerara sugar

Preheat the oven to 240°C/220°C fan.

Tip the oats, cinnamon, allspice and 2 tablespoons of the golden caster sugar into a large mixing bowl and mix well to coat the oats. Set aside.

In a bowl, whisk the miso into the custard.

Add the milk to the bowl with the oats, then scrape in the miso custard. Fold them through the oats, mixing well to combine. Set aside.

Dress the berries in the remaining golden caster sugar and the lemon zest and juice, and fold them carefully through the oat mixture, until evenly distributed.

Pour the mixture into a medium baking dish (about 20–25cm diameter), sprinkle the demerara sugar over and bake for 25–30 minutes, until the top is golden brown and the filling is bubbling.

Frozen berry fro-yo

Ice cream is always top in my book, but I rarely seem to have the time to organise myself into making a custard and waiting for it all to freeze. My simple berry fro-yo can be made in minutes – and eaten in seconds.

Serves 3

200g frozen mixed berries
200g full-fat extra-thick
   Greek yoghurt
2 tablespoons runny honey
1 teaspoon ground ginger
1 teaspoon allspice
1 teaspoon ground cardamom
1 tablespoon pomegranate seeds
a few fresh berries (optional),
   to decorate

Put the frozen berries, the yoghurt, 1 tablespoon of the honey and all the spices in a food processor and blitz them together for 20 seconds, until the mixture has the texture of thick whipped cream. Divide the fro-yo equally between three bowls, drizzle each one with the remaining honey and scatter over the pomegranate seeds. Serve straight away, decorated with a few fresh berries, if you wish.

Tahini-drizzled caramel bananas

Tahini caramel drizzled over anything is a winner, but this riff on regular caramelised bananas could just be life-changing. The fragrant cinnamon adds warmth, while the sesame seeds enhance the natural nuttiness of the tahini, making this an easy but elegant dessert.

Serves 2

55g caster sugar
1 teaspoon vanilla paste
1 tablespoon ground cinnamon
2 bananas, each peeled and
  sliced lengthways into 3
a knob of unsalted butter
1 tablespoon tahini
1 teaspoon sesame seeds

Warm the sugar, vanilla paste and cinnamon in a medium saucepan (it needs to be wide enough to fit the length of the bananas) over a medium heat, without stirring but swirling the pan from time to time, until a caramel forms (about 4–6 minutes). Place the banana slices into the pan, then stir them through the caramel to coat. Add the butter and leave it to melt for 1–2 minutes, until sumptuous and glossy.

Transfer the caramelised bananas to a plate, drizzle with the tahini and finish with a sprinkling of sesame seeds. (You can serve any caramel left in the pan on the side, if you like, for extra spoonfuls.)

Restoration

Restoration is all about fresher recipes that have an energy-boosting zing – the zing we sometimes need to get out of a slump and face the world. Never underestimate the power of good food.

French pickled onion soup

In my dreams I'm the kind of person who will spend hours creating a rich, satisfying, onion-filled, classic French onion soup, but, in reality, I simply do not have the time or patience for it. All is not lost, though. In this recipe I use finely sliced pickled onions, which transform the cooking time and add a tangy undertone to the dish. This is a deeply restorative alternative to France's original, if ever there was one.

Serves 2

30g unsalted butter
1 tablespoon olive oil
1 × 440g jar of strong pickled
  onions, drained and thinly
  sliced (reserve the liquid)
1 teaspoon caster sugar
50ml pickled onion juice (from
  the jar)
2 garlic cloves, grated
1 tablespoon plain flour
800ml hot beef stock, made
  with 2 jelly beef stock pots
a few flat-leaf parsley sprigs,
  leaves picked and chopped

Melt the butter with the olive oil in a medium saucepan over a medium heat. Add the sliced pickled onions, put the lid on the pan, and sweat the onions for 10 minutes, until soft.

Remove the lid, add the sugar and cook for 15 minutes more, stirring to ensure the sugar doesn't catch on the bottom of the pan and adding 1 tablespoon of the onion juice half way through, until the onions have a golden, caramelised colour.

Add the garlic, cook for 2 minutes, then add in the plain flour and stir well to cook out the flour.

Increase the heat and keep stirring as you gradually add the remaining pickled-onion juice, followed by the beef stock. Once it's all in, give everything a thorough stir, then cover the pan with the lid again and simmer for 10 minutes, until the soup is thick and reduced. Divide the soup between two bowls, then scatter equally with the parsley and serve.

Pickled vegetable salad

Simplicity is often the best way to enjoy vegetables, so for that reason there are just a few extra ingredients in this recipe, most of them already probably in your store cupboard. Make a dressing out of them and you will transform your veggies into mouth-tingling deliciousness.

Serves 2

For the dressing
1 tablespoon white miso
1 lime, zest and juice, plus
   optional extra wedges to serve
1cm piece of ginger root, peeled
   and grated
2 teaspoons English mustard
3 teaspoons malt vinegar
2 teaspoons maple syrup
1 tablespoon sherry vinegar
4 tablespoons good olive oil
salt and ground black pepper

For the salad
1 carrot, sliced into ribbons
2 spring onions, sliced into sticks
1 courgette, sliced into ribbons
1 cucumber, sliced into ribbons
1 red onion, sliced into half
   moons
a handful of coriander, leaves
   picked and roughly chopped

Mix all the ingredients for the dressing in a large bowl and whisk vigorously. Season generously with salt and pepper and stir to combine.

Add the vegetables and herbs into the dressing and leave them to marinate for 15 minutes, then serve with extra lime wedges for squeezing over, if you wish.

Tomatoes with chilli oil and yoghurt

*Try to find good-quality vine tomatoes for this dish – in my opinion, there is nothing
that captures a warm day in the Mediterranean quite as well as a flavourful tomato.
The other ingredients in this salad are specially selected to make those tomatoes sing:
chilli oil adds aromatic heat that's balanced out by the sharp lemon and creamy
yoghurt. Altogether, it's a simple dish that's not only full of flavour, but of summer, too.*

Serves 2

4 vine tomatoes, each cut
   into eight
2 teaspoons chilli oil
1 tablespoon maple syrup
2 tablespoons full-fat extra-thick
   Greek yoghurt
4 basil sprigs, roughly chopped
   (optional), plus a few whole
   leaves to garnish
1 lemon, zest and juice

Place the tomato wedges in a bowl and drizzle them with the chilli
oil. Add the maple syrup and toss the tomatoes until they're coated
in the sweet dressing.

Spread the yoghurt over a plate and sprinkle it with the chopped
basil, if using, and the lemon zest.

Pile the tomato wedges in the centre of the yoghurt, then finish
with a sprinkling of lemon juice to taste, and garnish with the
whole basil leaves.

Mango chutney baked cod with roasted okra

Mango chutney is given a starring role in this recipe. Both tart and sweet, it is an all-in-one pick-me-up that lends itself perfectly to the mild, flaky backdrop of baked cod.

Serves 2

2 tablespoons mango chutney
1 long red (Thai) chilli, deseeded
  and finely chopped, plus extra
  slices to serve
1 lime, zest and juice
1 tablespoon garam masala
4 tablespoons full-fat Greek
  yoghurt
2 × 180g skinless, boneless
  cod fillets
a few mint leaves, to serve

For the okra
10–12 pieces of okra (ladies'
  fingers)
1 tablespoon mild curry powder
1 tablespoon vegetable oil
salt

Preheat the oven to 180°C/160°C fan.

Place the mango chutney, chilli, lime zest and juice, garam masala and yoghurt into a mixing bowl and stir well to combine. Place the cod fillets into the bowl and turn them gently to coat them in the yoghurt mixture. Cover the bowl with a clean tea towel and leave the fish to marinate for 10 minutes at room temperature.

In the meantime, place the okra into a mixing bowl with the curry powder and oil and a generous pinch of salt. Turn them to coat and then arrange them on a baking tray lined with baking paper, neatly so that they form a bed for the cod.

Place the marinated cod fillets on top of the okra and transfer the baking tray to the oven. Bake the cod for 12 minutes, or until it is cooked through and the okra is tender. Scatter over the mint and extra chilli slices, to serve.

Gherkin sauce

There are those who keep the sliced gherkin in their burger and there are those who pull it out and put it on the side. I'm a keeper. In this preparation, I've reinvented gherkins into a sauce, with maple syrup, tomatoes and vinegar, to give a smooth, flavour-packed topping to slather over meat, fish or veg, as you fancy.

Makes 100ml

4 large, sweet-and-sour
  dill pickles
1 tablespoon maple syrup
2 tablespoons malt vinegar
2 large tomatoes

Add all of the ingredients to a food processor and pulse until completely combined and smooth.

If you don't have a food processor, you can chop the gherkins and tomatoes as finely as possible and mix them together with the maple syrup and vinegar in a bowl. Your sauce with have more texture, but sometimes that's no bad thing.

Umami beans

My take on classic baked beans, this recipe gives the family favourite an intensity makeover with the aniseed undertones from the tangy fennel. A good serving of gut-friendly garlic make these beans good for body and soul.

Serves 3

3 banana shallots, peeled
5 garlic cloves, peeled
3 tablespoons vegetable oil
1 teaspoon fennel seeds
10 fresh shiitake mushrooms
1 × 400g tin of black beans,
   drained and rinsed
1 × 400g tin of haricot beans,
   drained and rinsed
2 tablespoons tomato purée
1 teaspoon ground black pepper
2 teaspoons caster sugar
salt
slices of thickly buttered, warm
   toast, to serve
a few chive stems, finely
   chopped, to serve

Place the peeled shallots and garlic into a food processor and blitz until smooth. Season with a pinch of salt and add all the vegetable oil. Pulse again to mix thoroughly.

Place the mixture into a large saucepan and cover the pan with a lid. Cook over a low heat for 20 minutes, until the garlic is sweet-smelling and the mixture is pulpy. Remove the lid, stir in the fennel seeds and shiitakes and then replace the lid. Turn up the heat and cook for a further 5 minutes to give the seeds time to infuse the mixture.

Tip all the rinsed beans into the pan and mix well. Add the tomato purée, pepper and sugar and 150ml of water and stir well to combine. Cook for a further 10 minutes, until the beans are heated through and the mixture has thickened. Serve with warm buttered toast and sprinkled with chives.

Miso minestrone

Miso is well known as a source of umami and gut goodness, and minestrone is a well-known bowl of comfort. Put the two together and you get this fantastic recipe. I could say more, but that would be wasting valuable cooking time.

Serves 1

2 tablespoons olive oil
1 onion, finely chopped
2 garlic cloves, minced
1 carrot, finely chopped
5 dried shiitake mushrooms
1 tablespoon white miso
1 tablespoon dark soy sauce
500ml chicken stock
75g orzo

Heat the oil in a medium saucepan over a medium heat. When hot, add the onion, garlic and carrot and sweat for 7–9 minutes, until soft. Stir in the shiitake.

Whisk together the miso, soy sauce and chicken stock and add the mixture to the pan. Turn up the heat, bring the liquid to the boil, then add the orzo and cook for 9 minutes, until the pasta is tender. Ladle the minestrone into a bowl, and serve.

Kimchi cucumbers

Kimchi and cucumbers are two of my favourite things, both are really good for you, both are delicious. So why not bring them together in the style of Japanese smacked cucumbers. These are the perfect snack when you require goodness and flavour.

Serves 1

1 cucumber
80g kimchi
1 tablespoon light soy sauce
1 tablespoon maple syrup
1 teaspoon white wine vinegar

Put the cucumber in a food bag on your work surface, or place it on the surface and cover it with cling film. Lightly pound the cucumber with a rolling pin until it cracks and is slightly flattened (don't turn it to mush!). Remove it from the bag or remove the cling film and cut the cucumber into large, irregular chunks. Place these in a medium serving bowl and set aside.

Add the kimchi, soy sauce, maple syrup and vinegar into a small food processor and blitz them together until almost smooth.

Pour the kimchi marinade over the cucumber pieces in the bowl and chill for 2 hours before serving.

Kimchi salmon with ginger greens

Kimchi is full of gut-loving goodness, but more importantly its tangy flavour makes it a natural partner for fish. Baking it with salmon and serving with ginger-laced greens creates a healthy, flavour-packed meal for very little effort at all.

Serves 2

6 tablespoons kimchi, diced as
   finely as possible
½ teaspoon sesame oil
1 lime, zest and juice
¼ teaspoon white pepper
2 × 180g skinless, boneless
   salmon fillets
a few coriander leaves, to garnish

For the greens
2 heads of pak choi or 1 head
   of spring greens
1 tablespoon ginger paste
1 tablespoon garlic paste
1 tablespoon light soy sauce
1 tablespoon vegetable oil

To serve
a few coriander sprigs, for
   sprinkling
cooked white rice (optional)
crispy fried egg (optional)

Preheat the oven to 180°C/160°C fan.

Place the diced kimchi into a mixing bowl. Add the sesame oil and the lime zest and juice and mix well. Add the white pepper and then add the salmon, turning the fillets gently to coat them in the marinade. Cover the bowl with a clean tea towel and leave the salmon to marinate at room temperature for 10 minutes.

Meanwhile, in another bowl, mix together all the ingredients for the greens, making sure the greens themselves are well coated.

Place the salmon on a baking tray lined with baking paper and arrange the pak choi or spring greens around the sides of the fish. Transfer the baking tray to the oven and bake the fish and greens for 12 minutes, until the salmon is cooked through and the greens are lightly wilted.

Scatter over the coriander and serve the dish just as it is, or place it on a bed of rice with a crispy fried egg on top for something more substantial.

Chilli and tamarind cucumber

This simple cucumber salad is fresh and tart with intense flavours and makes a good, light lunch when you need something to wake up your taste buds and your spirits all at the same time.

Serves 2

1 large cucumber, sliced into
  1cm-thick rounds
salt
toasted sesame seeds, to serve

For the dressing
8 tablespoons malt vinegar
1 tablespoon kecap manis
  (sweet soy)
½ teaspoon dried chilli flakes
1 teaspoon tamarind paste
½ teaspoon sesame oil

Place the cucumber rounds into a large bowl and season them lightly with salt. Leave them for 10 minutes, then rinse them thoroughly in cold water to remove the salt. Pop the cucumber into a serving bowl.

In a separate bowl, mix together the ingredients for the dressing, then pour this over the cucumber. Leave the cucumber to sit for at least 10 minutes to take on the flavours of the dressing, then sprinkle over the sesame seeds to serve.

Sundried tomato fried eggs

Eggs and tomatoes are such good friends that it felt absolutely natural to fry these eggs on a sundried tomato base. The combination of creamy, runny yolks with tart, umami-rich tomatoes is topped with salty feta to enhance the flavours to perfection.

Serves 1

100g sundried tomatoes, finely
   chopped
6 basil leaves, finely chopped
2 eggs
20g feta cheese, crumbled

Combine the chopped sundried tomatoes and basil leaves in a bowl and add them to a medium frying pan (use one with a lid) set over a medium heat. Form the mixture into a large circle, flattening it down with the back of a spoon.

Crack the eggs into the mixture, place the lid on the pan and leave the eggs to cook for 3–4 minutes, then remove the lid and cook for a further 1 minute, until the whites are set but the yolks are still runny. Remove the pan from the heat and use a spatula to carefully transfer the eggs, with the tomato and basil base, to a plate. Sprinkle over the feta to finish.

Fennel salad

Fennel and orange make a classic combination. The flavours are fresh and bright, and in this case I've brought in saltiness from the olives and halloumi.

Serves 2

1 fennel bulb, very thinly sliced

1 red onion, thinly sliced into half
  moons

2 oranges, juice of 1 and skin and
  white pith removed, flesh cut
  into rounds for the other

4 tablespoons white wine or
  sherry vinegar

10 pitted green olives, thinly
  sliced

200g halloumi, cut into thick
  matchsticks

1 tablespoon nigella seeds,
  toasted

Combine the fennel and onion slices and scatter them over a serving plate. Set aside.

In a small mixing bowl, combine the orange juice and vinegar to make a dressing. Pour this over the fennel and onion salad, then artfully place the olives and orange rounds on top.

In a small frying pan, over a medium heat, fry the halloumi for 2–3 minutes, turning, until golden brown all over. Place the halloumi matchsticks on top of the salad and sprinkle over the nigella seeds to finish.

Wasabi pea and miso soup

There are gentle restoratives (when we need a hug in a bowl of food) and then there are restoratives that send power to the senses and so to the body – a bowl of get up and go. This deceptively simple soup is definitely the latter. Wasabi hits the trigeminal nerve with gusto, while the peas and miso combine for second bout of umami punch. Consider yourself energised.

Serves 2

2 tablespoons vegetable oil
1 onion, roughly chopped
1 tablespoon ginger paste
2 tablespoons white miso,
  diluted in 500ml boiling water
500g frozen peas, defrosted
1 tablespoon wasabi paste
10 mint leaves, plus extra to serve

Heat the oil in a large saucepan over a medium heat. Add the onions and the ginger paste and fry for 5–6 minutes, until the onion is softened but not coloured. Add the hot, diluted miso and turn off the heat. Add the peas, reserving a few for decoration, then add the wasabi and mint leaves. Using a stick blender, immediately blend the soup until it's smooth, then reheat it over a high heat for 2 minutes, until piping hot. Scatter over the reserved peas and the extra mint leaves and serve straight away.

Za'atar and sumac pesto

I've given a Middle Eastern twist to a Mediterranean classic in this recipe. Za'atar is my all-time favourite dried herb mixture (made from the dried za'atar herb, combined with sesame seeds, as well as dried sumac and other spices) – not just for its flavour, but also for its versatility and the way it can boost the citrus flavours in a dish. Serve this pesto stirred through pasta, scrambled eggs or boiled potatoes.

Makes 200ml

25g pine nuts, toasted
a large handful of basil leaves
2 tablespoons za'atar
1 tablespoon sumac
60g parmesan, grated
a large pinch of salt
1 large lemon, zest and juice
4 tablespoons olive oil

Tip the toasted pine nuts into a food processor, then add all the remaining ingredients except the olive oil. Whizz until the mixture is roughly chopped. Little by little, add the olive oil, whizzing between each addition, to give a spoonable mixture. Use just as you would any shop-bought pesto – over pasta, stirred through scrambled eggs or boiled new potatoes, and so much more!

Gochujang, ginger and avocado toast

If you thought that avocado toast was perfect just as it is, think again – my gochujang and ginger version is a whole new level. It retains the freshness you'd expect from such a dish, but adds foody superpower in its fiery warmth.

Serves 1

1 large avocado, peeled, destoned
   and mashed
1 large lime, zest and juice
1 tablespoon gochujang paste
5–7 coriander sprigs, chopped
a large pinch of freshly ground
   black pepper
2 slices of your favourite bread,
   toasted
ginger paste, for spreading
½ teaspoon nigella seeds,
   to garnish

Put the mashed avocado in a bowl, stir through the lime zest and loosen it with the juice. Stir through the gochujang paste, coriander and pepper until evenly combined.

Spread the slices of toast with a thin layer of ginger paste, then top them generously with the avocado mixture and sprinkle with the nigella seeds to garnish.

Green herb salsa

A simple salsa can bring restorative powers to any dish – the combination of herbs and vinegar in this one makes it an elixir worthy of drizzling on just about anything.

Makes 100ml

50g basil, leaves and stems
50g mint, leaves picked
50g coriander, leaves and stems
50g chives
2 large tomatoes
20ml malt vinegar
1 long green (Thai) chilli
  (optional), destemmed

Place all of the ingredients into a food processor and blitz until smooth. If you don't have a food processor, use a knife to chop all of the herbs as finely as you can and mix them in a bowl with the remaining ingredients – the sauce will have more texture, but sometimes that's no bad thing. The flavours are best when you serve the sauce immediately, but you can keep it in an airtight jar for up to 2 days in the fridge if needs be.

Toban djan, maple and soy longstem broccoli

Toban djan is a hot and spicy chilli bean paste, made using fermented broad beans. It adds definite zip when slathered over bitter green veg (in my case, longstem broccoli). Soy sauce brings salty intensity and the maple syrup brings sweetness to ensure that this is an all-round flavour hit from start to finish.

Serves 2

1 tablespoon toban djan
2 tablespoons maple syrup
1 tablespoon light soy sauce
½ teaspoon sesame oil
200g longstem broccoli, trimmed
50g roasted peanuts, crushed, to serve

Preheat the oven to 200°C/180°C fan.

Place the toban djan, maple, soy and sesame oil into a large mixing bowl and combine them with a spoon. Add the broccoli, turning it until it's thoroughly coated in the mixture.

Spread out the broccoli over a lined baking tray and place it in the oven for 15 minutes, until roasted and tender. Transfer the broccoli to a serving dish and scatter with the crushed peanuts to serve.

Cauliflower and potato coconut curry

Never underestimate the simple, restorative power of a curry. This cauliflower and coconut version sings with fresh flavours for an instant pick-me-up, without detracting from everything that is welcoming and familiar in a bowl of warm curry deliciousness.

Serves 2

4 shallots, finely diced
5 garlic cloves
1 lime, zested and quartered
2cm piece of ginger root, peeled
1 long red (Thai) chilli, destemmed, plus optional extra slivers to serve
1 long green (Thai) chilli, destemmed
1½ tablespoons garam masala
1 tablespoon medium curry powder
3 tablespoons vegetable oil
1 tablespoon ground coriander
1 cinnamon stick (about 10cm long)
1 × 400g tin of full-fat coconut milk
1 large potato (I like Maris Piper), peeled and cut into 2cm pieces
1 cauliflower, florets separated
2 tablespoons smooth peanut butter
100g coriander, finely chopped
salt
boiled jasmine rice, to serve

Put the shallots, garlic, lime zest, ginger, both chillies, garam masala, curry powder, oil, ground coriander and a sprinkle of salt into a food processor and blitz until completely smooth. Place the mixture into a large saucepan and add the cinnamon stick. Give everything a stir to make sure it doesn't stick to the bottom of the pan and then place the pan over a low heat for about 20 minutes, until the mixture smells sweet and aromatic.

Remove the cinnamon stick and then add the coconut milk and about 100ml of water and stir to combine. Add the potato, simmer over a low heat for 20 minutes, then add the cauliflower. Stir well and simmer for another 10 minutes. Finally, stir in the peanut butter and mix well until the sauce is combined. Remove the pan from the heat.

Stir half the chopped coriander through the curry, then ladle it into bowls and sprinkle with the remaining coriander to serve. Serve with boiled jasmine rice, the lime wedges for squeezing over, and sprinkled with slivers of extra red chilli, if you wish.

Pineapple, feta and coriander salad

I love using pineapple in my recipes – its tangy, tart flavour is mouthwatering and brightens up any dish. Combining it here with salty feta, umami-rich tomatoes and lively and fresh coriander makes this salad truly irresistible.

Serves 2

4 large tomatoes, sliced into
  wedges
1 pineapple, peeled, cored and
  sliced into 2cm-thick chunks
1 cucumber, halved lengthways
  and thinly sliced into half
  moons
1 baby gem lettuce, thinly sliced
2 red onions, finely sliced
200g feta, crumbled
10 mint leaves, shredded

For the dressing
4 tablespoons sherry vinegar
1 tablespoon pomegranate
  molasses or maple syrup
2 tablespoons good olive oil

Place the tomatoes, pineapple, cucumber, lettuce and red onions into a large mixing bowl and combine well. Set aside.

In a small bowl, combine the ingredients for the dressing, then pour the dressing over the salad and turn everything gently to fully coat.

Transfer the salad to a serving bowl or dish, scatter over the feta and mint leaves and serve.

Fridge-raid charred green veg with tahini sauce

I'm using broccoli, courgette and green pepper for my fridge-raid supper, but don't let me stop you if cauliflower and green beans – or anything else – are what's lurking in your fridge. This recipe is restorative because the tahini sauce adds plenty of creamy nuttiness that lifts the soul, and the whole dish comes with the satisfaction of no waste. Charring vegetables gives them a smoky warmth, which I love.

Serves 1–2

1 broccoli, florets separated
1 courgette, chopped into
  2–3cm chunks
1 green pepper, deseeded
  and cut into 2–3cm chunks
200g frozen peas
olive oil, for drizzling
za'atar, for sprinkling
salt and ground black pepper

For the tahini sauce
1 garlic clove, crushed
50g white tahini
50g full-fat extra-thick
  Greek yoghurt
1 lemon, zest and juice
¼ teaspoon sesame oil
1 teaspoon light soy sauce

Preheat the oven to 220°C/200°C fan.

Place all of the vegetables into a baking tray, mix them up and drizzle them with olive oil. Season with salt and pepper and place the tray in the oven. Roast the veg for 15–20 minutes, until the broccoli is beginning to brown lightly and everything is tender. Remove the baking tray from the oven, liberally scatter the veg with za'atar, and set aside while you make the sauce.

Place all the sauce ingredients in a medium mixing bowl and whisk well to combine (a balloon whisk is best for this to make sure everything is properly emulsified).

To serve, create a swirl of tahini sauce on each plate and pile high each serving with the veg.

Hot-and-sour prawn broth

Restoration and broth go hand in glove, just like hot and sour. This is a powerful bowl of goodness that will instantly lift your spirits.

Serves 2

400ml dashi stock
2cm ginger, peeled and finely
  chopped
2 garlic cloves, finely chopped
1 long red (Thai) chilli, finely
  chopped (deseeded if you want
  less heat)
½ teaspoon ground white pepper
6 dried shiitake mushrooms
½ teaspoon sesame oil
1 teaspoon light soy sauce
1 teaspoon rice vinegar or white
  wine vinegar
1 broccoli head, florets separated
10 shelled large king prawns
100g dried vermicelli noodles
2 large eggs
a few coriander sprigs, leaves
  picked
lime wedges, to serve

Pour the dashi stock into a large saucepan, then add the ginger, garlic, chilli and white pepper. Place the pan over a low heat and bring the seasoned stock to a simmer.

Leave to simmer for 10 minutes, then add the dried mushrooms, sesame oil, soy sauce and vinegar. Simmer for 5 minutes more, or until the mushrooms are fully rehydrated and soft. Add the broccoli florets and king prawns and continue to simmer gently for 6–8 minutes, until the prawns are pink and cooked through.

Add the noodles, breaking them up with a wooden spoon, if you like, and then crack in both eggs, stirring them through the broth so that the eggs break up into small pieces. Scatter over the coriander leaves, and serve with lime wedges for squeezing in to taste.

Ultimate chicken noodle soup

This recipe gives a classic chicken noodle soup the ultimate makeover – made even better with the gift of time. The long, slow cooking leaves the ingredients to simmer and stew and impart all their goodness throughout the broth. There's something very satisfying about tucking into a bowl of soup that has been bubbling away, filling your kitchen with its flavours even before it hits your taste buds. I've used noodles and dumplings in this recipe, but you can leave out the dumplings, if you wish; and the noodles too for something even lighter.

Serves 4

1 small chicken, portioned into
  6 pieces
2 carrots, cut into 1cm chunks
1 onion, cut into 3cm chunks
1 large swede, peeled and cut into
  3cm chunks
1 leek, sliced into 2cm rounds
2 tablespoons white miso
1 litre chicken stock
3 garlic cloves
3 cloves
1 tablespoon black peppercorns
½ handful of marjoram (optional),
  leaves picked
1 × 220g tin of pease pudding
200g thin dried egg noodles
  (about 4 nests)
a small handful of chives, finely
  chopped, to serve

For the dumplings
50g suet
100g plain flour
¼ teaspoon ground white pepper
½ teaspoon salt

Put all the chicken ingredients except for the noodles and pease pudding into a large saucepan. Give everything a good stir to make sure that the miso is mixed into the stock, and then place the pan over a medium–low heat. Bring the liquid to a simmer, then simmer for at least 1 hour, until the chicken is cooked through and the meat is falling off the bone.

When the hour is almost up, make the dumplings. Combine the suet, flour, pepper and salt in a bowl and slowly incorporate 3 tablespoons of water, until the mixture comes together in a sticky dough. Divide the dough into 4 equal portions and set aside.

Once the chicken is ready, add the tin of pease pudding to the soup, stir, then pop in the dumplings. Put the lid on the pan and simmer for 10 minutes. Then, break up the noodles, remove the lid and add them to the soup. Replace the lid and simmer for a further 5 minutes, until the dumplings have steamed in the pan and are cooked through and the noodles are tender.

Don't worry about removing the bones from the soup – ladle everything into bowls, scatter with the chives and enjoy, discarding the bones as you go.

Sumac, chilli and ginger almonds

This all-day nibble is a stunning way to get almonds, which are rich in antioxidants, protein and healthy fats, into your diet. Ginger brings fiery heat and Middle Eastern sumac adds a lemon twang.

Makes 2–3 servings

2 tablespoons maple syrup
1 teaspoon sumac
1 tablespoon chilli oil
2.5cm piece of ginger root, finely
  grated
75g whole, unblanched almonds

Preheat the oven to 200°C/180°C fan.

In a bowl, mix together everything except the nuts until combined.

Add the nuts to the bowl and stir them until they are fully coated in the sticky spice mixture.

Tip the coated nuts into a roasting tin, spread them out into a single layer, then roast them for 10 minutes, until darkened. Leave them to cool and harden – they will fuse together in the process to create a sort of brittle. Once the brittle has cooled, use your hands to break it apart into individual almonds again. The nuts will store in an airtight jar for 3–5 days.

Pomegranate baked figs
with orange mascarpone

Pomegranate molasses transforms these baked figs into a sticky, sweet-and-sour, flavour-packed dessert. Exactly what any of us needs to see us through to bedtime.

Serves 2

2 tablespoons pomegranate
  molasses
½ teaspoon vanilla paste
1 teaspoon runny honey
4 ripe figs
pomegranate seeds, to serve

For the orange mascarpone
150g mascarpone
1 orange, zest and juice
½ teaspoon orange blossom
  water (optional)

Preheat the oven to 180°C/160°C fan.

Mix together the pomegranate molasses, vanilla and honey in a bowl. Place the figs snugly into a baking dish, drizzle over the pomegranate mixture, and bake them for 25 minutes, until they are soft and have started to burst.

Meanwhile, make the orange mascarpone. In a small bowl, whip the mascarpone with the orange zest and juice, and the orange blossom water if you're using it, until fully combined and fluffy. Set aside until the figs are ready.

To serve, divide the mascarpone equally between two serving dishes, then top with the figs (they look pretty halved rather than whole, if you prefer). Finish with a scattering of pomegranate seeds.

Tamarind-roasted strawberry compôte over frozen yoghurt

Tart tamarind lifts the sweetness of the roasted strawberries in this simple dessert. Serving the compôte over the icy chill of frozen yogurt gives your senses plenty to wake up for (and the strawberries are delicious over yoghurt straight from the fridge, too).

Serves 2

100g full-fat extra-thick Greek
  yoghurt
250g fresh strawberries,
  quartered
2 tablespoons caster sugar
1 tablespoon tamarind paste
1 lime, zest and juice
a few mint leaves (optional), very
  finely chopped, to serve

Put the yogurt in the freezer for 1 hour before you intend to serve.

When you're ready to make the compôte, preheat the oven to 200°C/180°C fan and line a baking tray with baking paper.

Tip the strawberries into a mixing bowl and sprinkle over the sugar. Add the tamarind and the lime zest and juice and use a spoon to mix everything gently together, making sure the strawberries are well coated. Leave them to marinate for 10 minutes, then tip them on to the lined baking tray and roast them for 15 minutes, until they are soft and sticky. Remove from the heat and leave to cool until warm but not hot.

Remove the yoghurt from the freezer and scoop it equally into two bowls (or spoon it into your bowls straight from the fridge). Divide the warm compôte between the bowls, sprinkle with the mint (if using), and serve straight away.

Passion fruit and lime Eton mess

Nothing puts tropical sunshine in a bowl like passion fruit, vanilla, lime and coconut. Use them as a twist on a quintessentially English summertime dessert and it's like a worldwide holiday all in one. (I'll let you in on a secret – I think this version of an Eton mess is better than the classic.)

Serves 2

4 tablespoons coconut flakes
250ml double cream
1 tablespoon caster sugar
1 tablespoon vanilla paste
2 limes, zest and juice
2 passion fruit, pulp scooped out
4 meringue nests, crushed
a few mint leaves, to serve

Preheat the oven to 200°C/180°C fan.

Scatter the coconut flakes over a baking tray and toast them in the oven for about 4 minutes, or until just golden. Remove them from the oven and set aside.

In a large bowl, whisk together the double cream, sugar, vanilla and lime zest until the mixture forms soft peaks. Set aside.

In a separate bowl, mix together the passion-fruit pulp and lime juice.

To assemble, in each glass create equal layers of cream, crushed meringue and passion fruit (in that order), twice – so, six layers in total. Sprinkle over the coconut flakes and finish with the mint leaves, to serve.

Miso, white chocolate and lemon butter cookies

Inspired by my own Life Kitchen classic 'Miso white chocolate with frozen berries', these simple cookies make for a superb mid-afternoon energy boost when you need a sugar hit to power you through until suppertime.

Makes 10 cookies

180g self-raising flour
75g demerara sugar
zest of 3 lemons
50g white chocolate chips
½ teaspoon white miso
4 tablespoons vegetable oil
1 egg yolk
3 teaspoons poppy seeds

Place all of the ingredients except the poppy seeds into a mixing bowl and use your hands to combine them into a smooth dough. Refrigerate the dough for 20 minutes to firm up.

Preheat oven to 200°C/180°C fan.

Tip the poppy seeds on to a shallow plate. Remove the dough from the fridge and divide it into 10 equal pieces. Form each piece into a ball and roll it in the poppy seeds to give an even coating. Place the balls on to a lined baking tray, spacing them well apart, as you go.

Transfer the baking tray to the oven and bake the cookies for 10 minutes, until they have spread and are golden. Remove them from the oven and transfer them to a wire rack to cool. They will keep in an airtight container for up to 3 days (if you can resist them that long!).

Coconut and pandan chia pudding

Pandan is a fragrant plant from Southeast Asia, the leaves of which are used as a grassy, vanilla-like flavouring in many dishes from the region. Here, I've used pandan flavouring (widely available online or in Asian supermarkets) as the twist in this easy-to-assemble, but delicious pudding. Mix it up, leave it overnight and enjoy it straight from the fridge the following day (or even up to three days later). Winner.

Serves 2

60g chia seeds
220ml coconut milk from
  a carton (not a tin)
1 tablespoon maple syrup,
  plus extra to drizzle
a dash of pandan flavouring
  (a little goes a long way)

To serve
1 banana
a few blueberries (optional)

Combine the chia, coconut milk, maple syrup and pandan flavouring in a bowl. Divide the mixture equally between two serving glasses and cover the tops with foil or re-useable wrap. Refrigerate for 6 hours, or ideally overnight.

To serve, slice a little of the banana and use the slices to top the pudding, along with a few blueberries, if you wish.

Pleasure

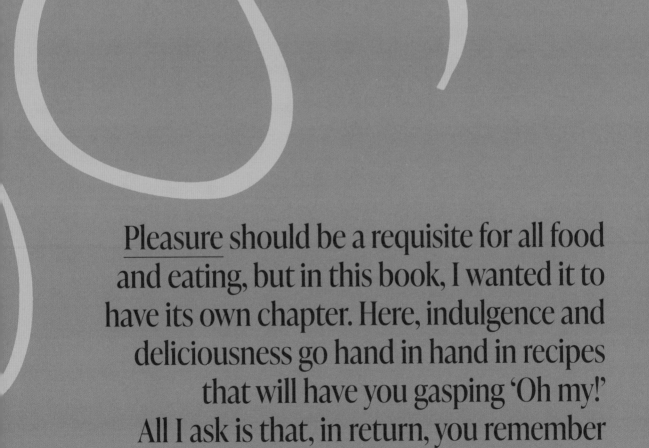

Pleasure should be a requisite for all food and eating, but in this book, I wanted it to have its own chapter. Here, indulgence and deliciousness go hand in hand in recipes that will have you gasping 'Oh my!' All I ask is that, in return, you remember one thing: you deserve it.

Parmesan and vinegar potatoes

Potatoes, parmesan and vinegar – is there a more heavenly combination? This trifecta of delights is the ultimate, tangy umami hit.

Serves 2–3 (or more as a snack)

500g new potatoes
olive oil, for drizzling
4 tablespoons red wine vinegar
80g parmesan, grated
salt

Bring a medium saucepan of salted water to the boil. Add the potatoes and boil them for 20 minutes, until tender. Drain the potatoes and spread them over a baking tray. Drizzle them with olive oil, then, using the flat bottom of a clean bowl, press down on them hard to smash them out of their skins. Sprinkle with salt to season and set aside while you heat the grill to high.

When the grill is ready, put the baking tray under the heat and leave the potatoes for about 7 minutes to start crisping. Then, drizzle over the vinegar and return them to the grill to crisp up for a further 8 minutes.

Remove the potatoes from the grill and sprinkle them all over with the parmesan. Put them back under the grill again and cook for a further 10 minutes, until the parmesan coating is golden and crispy. Serve immediately.

Plum and ginger sticky lamb chops with coriander yoghurt

Plum and ginger create an unctuous, sticky marinade that transforms lamb chops into these pleasure-packed delights. Slather the chops generously in the coriander yoghurt for the full flavour hit.

Serves 2

6 lamb chops
1 tablespoon ground coriander
¼ tablespoon ground white
   pepper
1 tablespoon ginger paste
1 tablespoon garlic paste
2 tablespoons any neutral oil
   (such as sunflower or rapeseed)
3 tablespoons plum sauce (I like
   the brand Healthy Boy)
salt
4 plums, destoned and halved,
   to serve

For the coriander yoghurt
150g full-fat extra-thick Greek
   yoghurt
50g coriander, finely chopped,
   plus extra to garnish

Place the lamb chops into a mixing bowl and add the ground coriander, white pepper, and ginger and garlic pastes and leave the chops to marinate for at least 10 minutes, or even overnight if you wish (in that case, cover the bowl and place the lamb in the fridge).

Meanwhile (or on the day you intend to cook), make the yoghurt simply by combining the yoghurt and the coriander in a bowl. Set aside.

To cook, place a large frying pan over medium–high heat. Add the oil and when it's hot, gently lay the chops into the pan. Cook them for 2 minutes, then turn them over and cook them for 1 minute more. Spoon the plum sauce over the chops and lightly shake the pan or use tongs to move the chops around to make sure they're fully coated. Season with salt to taste.

Spoon the yoghurt equally over two serving plates and divide the chops between them. Add the plum halves and sprinkle over some extra chopped coriander, to finish.

Late-night tuna pasta

There are some nights (particularly late ones) when only tuna pasta will do. This version is transformed with fiery, fragrant harissa and loaded with salty olives. It's not a tuna pasta for the fainthearted – it's for the thrillseeker that lies within.

Serves 2

200g tuna fillet, cut into 3cm
   pieces (or use a tin of tuna
   flakes in springwater, drained)
2 tablespoons vegetable oil
2 shallots, finely chopped
4 garlic cloves, crushed
1 tablespoon rose harissa paste
1 tablespoon capers, drained
100g pitted green or black olives
1 × 400g tin of cherry tomatoes
1 lemon, zest and juice
200g dried spaghetti
salt and ground black pepper
grated parmesan or pecorino
   (optional), to serve

Lightly season the tuna chunks with salt and pepper and set aside (if you're using tinned tuna, season that now, too). Put a large saucepan of well-salted water on to boil (this is for the spaghetti, but don't add the pasta yet).

Heat the oil in a frying pan over a medium heat, then add the shallots and garlic and fry for 3–4 minutes, until softened. Add the harissa, the tuna chunks (fresh or tinned) and the capers and olives and cook for a further 3–4 minutes, until the tuna begins to get some colour. Add the tomatoes and the lemon zest and juice and stir everything together. Keep warm.

Add the pasta to the boiling water and cook it according to the packet instructions, until al dente. Before draining the pasta, take one small ladleful of the cooking water and add it into the tuna and tomato sauce, stirring well to combine. Drain the pasta and add it to the sauce, mixing well to make sure it's all coated.

Divide the pasta and sauce between two bowls, and serve it with a generous grating of parmesan or pecorino on top, if you wish.

Red pepper and green chilli paratha

A paratha is a flaky Indian flat bread. It is simple to make from scratch, if you feel inclined, but I'm using shop-bought here because this chapter is all about pleasure – and in this case, that means delicious food in speedy minutes. These cheesy, chilli-packed parathas are guaranteed to hit the spot every time.

Serves 1

1 roasted red pepper from a jar, roughly chopped
1 green chilli, roughly chopped (deseeded if you want less heat)
50g extra-mature cheddar, grated
50g brie, chopped
1 teaspoon za'atar
2 coriander sprigs, finely chopped
1 paratha

Preheat the grill to medium.

Combine the pepper, chilli, cheeses and za'atar in a bowl with a fork, then add the coriander and mix through.

Lay the paratha on your work surface and spoon the mixture over the surface to cover in an even layer.

Heat a dry, oven-proof frying pan on a medium heat and when it's hot, carefully slide the paratha into the pan and cook it for 3–4 minutes, until the cheeses begin to melt. Then, remove the pan from the heat and place it under the grill for 2–3 minutes, until the topping is golden and the cheese is deliciously oozy and melted.

Transfer the flat bread to a plate and cut it into 4 wedges to serve.

Miso, mushroom and parmesan crumble

There's so much more to a crumble than the sweet dessert after a Sunday roast (although that's good, too) – in fact, a savoury crumble feels like pure indulgence. The miso, mushroom and parmesan ramp up the savoury flavours in this recipe, giving the crumble a depth that a million times outstrips its simplicity.

Serves 2

75g unsalted butter
1 teaspoon white miso
1 leek, thinly sliced
100g chestnut mushrooms,
  chopped
4 tablespoons double cream
salt and ground black pepper

For the crumble
50g unsalted butter
100g plain flour
2–3 thyme sprigs, leaves picked
75g parmesan, grated

Preheat the oven to 200°C/180°C fan.

Put the 75g of butter and the miso in a frying pan over a medium heat. When the butter has melted, add the leek and cook for 7 minutes, until the slices have collapsed and are soft but not coloured. Add the mushrooms, season with a good pinch of salt, and sizzle for 7 minutes, until they are browned. Season with pepper.

Transfer the mixture to a medium baking dish (about 20–25cm diameter) and stir through the double cream. Set aside while you make the crumble.

In a bowl, using your fingertips, rub the 50g of butter into the flour until you have a breadcrumb-like texture. Mix through the thyme leaves and parmesan.

Scatter the crumble evenly over the mushroom mixture and bake the crumble for 20 minutes, until the top is golden and the filling is bubbling up around the edges.

Kimchi and cheddar quesadillas

This is a personal favourite among the recipes in this book. Kimchi brings acidity and crunch to the luxuriousness of the strong cheddar. To me, there is always something deeply indulgent about a quesadilla – oozy, flavoursome cheese, laced with herbs and vibrantly tangy from the other ingredients, which is sandwiched between flat breads and ready in a flash. Pure pleasure.

Serves 1

4 tablespoons kimchi, chopped
100g extra-mature cheddar, grated
4 coriander sprigs, finely chopped
2 spring onions, finely chopped
4 small tortillas
4 tablespoons olive oil
lime wedges, to serve

Mix together the kimchi, cheddar, coriander and spring onion in a bowl until all the ingredients are evenly distributed.

Place the tortillas on your work surface and spread the mixture evenly over the surface of each. Fold each tortilla in half, to make a half-moon shape.

Heat half the oil in a medium frying pan over a medium heat. Fry each tortilla for 2–3 minutes per side, until golden all over and the cheese is melted, replenishing the oil as necessary. Serve with lime wedges for squeezing over.

Marmite, roasted onion and cannellini dip

Love it or hate it, Marmite is flavour-packed and umami-rich. In this recipe, I've roasted onions and cannellini beans with thyme and lemon to transform them into the best dip you'll ever have. Those strong savoury notes will keep you coming back for more – you've been warned.

Serves 2

2 tablespoons Marmite
1 × 400g tin of cannellini beans, drained (reserve the liquid)
1 onion, cut into 8 wedges
a handful of thyme sprigs, leaves picked
1 lemon, zest and juice
2 tablespoons crème fraîche
1 tablespoon maple syrup

Preheat oven to 200°C/180°C fan.

Mix together the Marmite and the liquid from the tin of beans until combined.

Place the onion wedges in a roasting tin with the beans and thyme sprigs, then pour over the Marmite mixture. Turn the onions to coat them fully. Roast the onion wedges for 45 minutes, until they are soft and dark, then remove them from the oven and stir through the lemon zest and juice.

Transfer two-thirds of the onion and bean mixture to a blender. Add the crème fraîche and maple syrup and blitz until smooth. Transfer the purée to a bowl and top with the remaining onion and bean mixture. Serve as a dip for crudités or lightly steamed veg (such as asparagus), or as a thick soup.

Roasted tomatoes on hummus

Heat and acidity are all you need to transform a humble tomato into something truly decadent. In this recipe, tomatoes are roasted to intensify their flavour and paired with smoked hummus to hit every flavour note on the palate.

Serves 2

a couple of handfuls of cherry
  tomatoes
1 teaspoon white miso
3 tablespoons good olive oil
1 tablespoon red wine vinegar
1 teaspoon fennel seeds
1 teaspoon sumac
100g smoked hummus
1 tablespoon za'atar

Preheat oven to 200°C/180°C fan.

Mix the tomatoes with the miso, 2 tablespoons of the olive oil, and the vinegar, fennel seeds and sumac in a roasting dish. Place the dish in the oven and roast the tomatoes for 45 minutes, until they are collapsed, sticky and charred in places.

Spread the hummus over a serving plate, drizzle it with the remaining olive oil and sprinkle it with the za'atar. Pile the roasted tomatoes on top to serve.

Kimchi baked eggs and Marmite soldiers

Can anything bring more pleasure than Marmite soldiers? Especially when they are there to dip in runny yolk. This is an elevated classic – you've had eggs baked in a tomato-y sauce, but add probiotic-rich kimchi and the dish becomes fiery, fragrant and good for you – no questions asked.

Serves 1

3 tablespoons kimchi
1 teaspoon white miso
1 × 400g tin of chopped
  tomatoes
2 eggs
1 slice of sourdough bread
1 tablespoon Marmite
a few coriander leaves, chopped
1 lemon, zest and juice

Place a small frying pan (use one with a lid) over a high heat and add the kimchi and miso. Fry for 3 minutes, then add the tomatoes. Reduce the heat to medium–high and leave them to bubble away for 10–15 minutes, until the sauce is reduced and thick. Using the back of a spoon, make two wells in the tomato mixture and crack 1 egg into each. Place the lid on the pan and cook the eggs for 4–5 minutes, until the whites of the eggs are cooked, but the yolks are still runny.

Meanwhile, toast the sourdough, then spread it with the Marmite and slice it into soldiers.

Remove the pan from the heat, scatter over the coriander and lemon zest and drizzle over the lemon juice. Serve scooped into a bowl – or straight from the pan (this is meant to be pure pleasure, after all) – with the soldiers for dipping.

Pomegranate chilli-glazed halloumi

Baked halloumi is a classic dish for a new era of dining. My version brings together the tangy sweetness of pomegranate molasses with chilli, mustard and lime. The result is a dazzler for the palate.

Serves 2

3 tablespoons pomegranate
  molasses
1 green chilli, chopped (deseeded
  if you want less heat)
1 tablespoon olive oil
1 tablespoon wholegrain mustard
1 × 225g block of halloumi, sliced
juice of 1 lime
2 tablespoons pomegranate
  seeds
a small handful of mint leaves,
  finely chopped, to serve

Preheat the oven to 200°C/180°C fan.

In a small baking dish, mix together the pomegranate molasses, chilli, olive oil and mustard to form a loose paste. Add the halloumi turning to cover it generously in the paste.

Bake the cheese, uncovered, for 25 minutes, then sprinkle over the lime juice and scatter with the pomegranate seeds and finely chopped mint, to serve.

Cheese and chutney galette

Cheese, chutney and pastry – all you need for a night in on the sofa in complete, homespun contentment.

Serves 3

1 × 320g sheet of ready-rolled
   shortcrust pastry
5 tablespoons red onion chutney
1 whole camembert, sliced
1 egg, beaten
1 teaspoon fennel seeds
3 tablespoons chopped walnuts
3 flat-leaf parsley sprigs, finely
   chopped

Preheat the oven to 180°C/160°C fan.

Lay the pastry sheet, with its baking paper, on a baking tray with a long side closest to you. Spread the chutney over the pastry, leaving a 2cm border around the edge, and add the slices of camembert on top, spacing them evenly over the filling.

Roughly fold up the sides and edges of the pastry to create a rim for the filling, then brush the edges with the beaten egg. Sprinkle the fennel seeds over the crust, letting them stick to the egg wash.

Bake the galette for 25 minutes, until the edges are golden brown and the cheese has melted. Remove it from the oven, sprinkle it with the walnuts and parsley, and serve.

Curried mushroom pie

Mushroom pie is one of my favourite things. In this version, miso ups the natural umami-ness of the mushrooms, which soak up flavour from the mild curry powder. This is a mouthwateringly delicious pastry-encased delight.

Serves 2

a knob of unsalted butter, plus
   extra for greasing
2 spring onions, finely chopped
25g porcini mushroom,
   rehydrated in 300ml boiling
   water
75g mixed mushrooms, sliced
3 tarragon sprigs, leaves picked
1 tablespoon mild curry powder
1 teaspoon light miso
1 x 320g sheet of ready-rolled
   puff pastry
1 egg, beaten with a drop of
   whole milk
1 teaspoon thyme leaves

Melt the butter in a medium frying pan over a medium heat. Add the spring onions and fry them for 2–3 minutes, until soft.

Drain the porcini mushrooms, retaining the liquid for later, then add all the mushrooms to the pan. Increase the heat to high and fry for 3–5 minutes, stirring to combine, until the mushrooms have started to take on a little colour. Add the tarragon leaves, fry, stirring, for 2–3 minutes, then add the curry powder, miso and mushroom soaking liquid. Leave the filling to bubble away for 7–9 minutes, until reduced and thickened. Leave it to cool.

While the filling is cooling, preheat the oven to 180°C/160°C fan and grease two medium pie dishes (each 15–20cm diameter) with a little butter. Lay the pastry sheet out on your work surface and cut it in half. Cut each half into two pieces, of one-third and two-thirds. Use the larger two pieces of pastry to line the pie dishes, pressing the pastry into the corners of the bottom of the pie dish and trimming to neaten the top edge as necessary.

Divide the cooled mushroom mixture between the dishes, filling each almost to the top. Use a little of the egg wash to brush the edges and then top with the remaining pieces of pastry to create a lid. Press the edges of the lid down onto the base with your fingers to seal and cut a small hole into the top of each pie.

Brush the pies all over with egg wash, sprinkle with the thyme leaves and place pies in the oven. Bake them for 20–22 minutes, until the filling is piping hot and pie tops are golden.

Sauerkraut pancakes
with harissa and maple drizzle

Gut goodness and pancakes don't usually end up in the same sentence, but I like to change things. I've added sauerkraut to this batter for a microbiome boost and drizzled the pancakes with maple and harissa sauce to keep my signature flavours – powerfully delicious.

Serves 1

120g plain flour
½ teaspoon baking powder
½ teaspoon bicarbonate of soda
½ teaspoon sea salt
100ml buttermilk
1 egg
100ml whole milk
2 teaspoons vegetable oil (such as sunflower or rapeseed)
3 tablespoons sauerkraut

For the sauce
1 teaspoon rose harissa paste
1 teaspoon white miso
3 tablespoons maple syrup

Mix the flour, baking powder, bicarbonate of soda and salt in a bowl. In a separate bowl mix the buttermilk, egg and milk until combined. Gradually add the dry ingredients to the bowl with the wet ingredients and whisk everything together until smooth. Set aside.

In a bowl, whisk together the sauce ingredients and set aside.

Heat 1 teaspoon of the vegetable oil in a small frying pan over a medium heat. When it's hot, pour in enough batter to evenly coat the bottom of the pan and cook the pancake for about 2 minutes, until bubbles appear on the surface. Place 1 tablespoon of the sauerkraut into the batter, covering the surface of the pancake and gently pressing it down. Flip the pancake and cook for a further 2 minutes, until both sides are golden. Transfer the cooked pancake to a warm plate, and repeat for the remaining batter and another tablespoon of the sauerkraut.

Stack the second pancake on top of the first, top the stack with the remaining sauerkraut and then drizzle the stack with the miso maple sauce, to serve.

Kimchi Caesar salad

A classic is a classic for a reason, but my version of a Caesar salad, with kimchi, excels in ways the original never thought possible. Not only does the kimchi add a microbiome twist, it's packed with fiery flavour.

Serves 1

2 garlic cloves, finely grated
3 anchovies, finely chopped
2 tablespoons mayonnaise
50g parmesan, finely grated
2 tablespoons good olive oil
2 tablespoons kimchi pickling
  liquid
1 small head of romaine lettuce,
  washed and separated
2 tablespoons kimchi, roughly
  chopped
1 slice of sourdough bread, crusts
  removed, toasted and cut into
  cubes

Whisk the garlic, anchovies, mayonnaise and parmesan in a large bowl with the olive oil. Stir in the 2 tablespoons of kimchi liquid to make a dressing.

Add the lettuce leaves to the bowl and toss them with the dressing, then transfer them to a serving plate. Scatter the chopped kimchi over the lettuce, then scatter over the cubed sourdough toast. Serve immediately.

Brown butter and fennel seed sausage pasta

What's better than butter? Browned butter with its notes of sweet caramel. Pair that with sausage meat and fennel seeds, and you have the makings of the ultimately indulgent pasta dish.

Serves 1

100g of your favourite dried
  pasta
1 tablespoon neutral oil (such
  as sunflower or rapeseed)
1 sausage, skinned and chopped
  or crumbled
1 teaspoon fennel seeds
50g unsalted butter
3 tablespoons double cream
3 flat-leaf parsley sprigs, leaves
  and tender stems finely
  chopped, plus optional extra
  to serve
1 lemon, zest and juice
50g parmesan, grated

Bring a saucepan of well-salted water to the boil. Add the pasta and cook it according to the packet instructions, until al dente.

Meanwhile, heat the oil in a medium frying pan over a medium heat. When hot, add the sausage meat and the fennel seeds and fry for 2–3 minutes, until the meat begins to colour. Add the butter and fry it for 2–3 minutes – it will turn amber in this time. Add the double cream, parsley, lemon zest and juice and 5 tablespoons of the pasta cooking water. Reduce the heat to low and stir the sauce, cooking for about 3–4 minutes, until thickened to the consistency of double cream. Drain the cooked pasta and add it to the sauce, stirring it through to coat. Finish by sprinkling over the parmesan, and a little extra parsley, if you wish.

Oven chips with comté cheese sauce

Pleasure doesn't necessarily mean full of effort – in fact, sometimes the most pleasurable eating is when the cooking part has been simplest of all. This recipe is 'simple' personified – and it is my take on a classic Northern dish of cheesy chips.

Serves 1

150g chunky oven chips
1 tablespoon unsalted butter
1 tablespoon plain flour
1 teaspoon wholegrain mustard
½ teaspoon ground cumin
150ml whole milk
100g comté, grated
ground black pepper

Preheat the oven to 200°C/180°C fan and cook the chips according to the packet instructions, until golden and crispy.

Meanwhile, in a small saucepan over medium heat, melt the butter and flour together to form a paste. Cook the paste for 1–2 minutes, until it begins to brown (this cooks out the floury flavour), then whisk in the mustard and cumin. Cook for a further 1 minute, then gradually incorporate the milk, whisking continuously after each addition, until the sauce has a semi-loose consistency. Add the comté and stir with a wooden spoon until it's melted. Season with pepper and keep the sauce warm until the chips are done.

Once the chips are ready, transfer the sauce into a dipping bowl, then season them both with more black pepper, if you wish – and then, dunk away!

Red onion marmalade cacio e pepe

This is cacio e pepe, a classic Italian pasta dish, but with sticky red onion marmalade as the base. Need I say more? Okay, I will. This deeply unctuous dish is literally peppered with trigeminal-nerve-stimulating condiment that adds a nose-tingling, darting lift to the pasta. Ultimate pleasure.

Serves 2

100g orzo
2 tablespoons tricolour (black, red and green) peppercorns, finely ground
1 heaped tablespoon unsalted butter
2 tablespoons red onion marmalade
50g parmesan, grated, plus optional extra to serve

Bring a saucepan of well-salted water to the boil. Add the pasta and cook according to the packet instructions, until al dente (about 7–8 minutes).

While the orzo is cooking, toast the finely ground peppercorns in a dry frying pan over a medium heat for 2–3 minutes, until aromatic. Add the butter, let it melt, then stir in the red onion marmalade to combine. Remove the pan from the heat.

A couple of minutes before the pasta is ready, remove 1 large mugful of pasta cooking water and gradually stir it into the sauce. Put the pan of sauce back over a medium heat and leave the mixture to reduce for about 4 minutes, until thickened to a loose sauce consistency (you want it so that it will cling to the pasta, but not so loose that it will run off – think single cream).

Meanwhile, reserve another mugful of pasta cooking water and then drain the cooked pasta in a colander.

Once the sauce has reduced, add the parmesan and stir it in so that it melts.

Mix the orzo into the sauce until fully coated. If it all looks too dry, gradually add the reserved pasta water and stir again, until the orzo has a luxurious, creamy coating. Transfer the pasta to a bowl and top with extra parmesan, if you wish.

Harissa and shiitake mac 'n' cheese

There are few foodie pleasures greater than a luxurious bowl of macaroni and cheese. My version has North African harissa paste, umami-packed shiitake mushrooms and crunchy Panko breadcrumbs to add heaps of flavour and texture to all that luxury.

Serves 2

200g macaroni (or other dried
    pasta)
1 tablespoon rose harissa paste
a knob of unsalted butter
1 tablespoon plain flour
20g dried shiitake mushrooms,
    rehydrated in 100ml water
100ml whole milk
100g extra-mature cheddar,
    grated
50g mozzarella (from a ball),
    grated
50g Panko breadcrumbs

Bring a saucepan of well-salted water to the boil. Add the pasta and cook according to the packet instructions, until al dente. Drain and set aside.

Preheat the oven to 200°C/180°C fan.

Melt the harissa and butter together in a medium saucepan over a medium heat. Add the flour, stirring to form a paste, then leave the flour to cook out for 1–2 minutes (this helps it to lose its floury flavour). Add the rehydrated mushrooms, reserving the soaking liquid. Cook for 1 minute, then gradually add the soaking liquid and milk, stirring continuously between each addition, until the mixture is fully combined to a smooth sauce. Add both cheeses, stir until melted, then fold in the cooked pasta, until it is fully coated in the sauce.

Tip the cheesy pasta mixture into a medium baking dish (about 20–25cm diameter), top with the Panko breadcrumbs and bake for 30 minutes, until golden and bubbling.

Marmite and sesame French toast

The savoury notes of French toast are given a lift in this easy recipe that's perfect for breakfast or lunch. Sesame seeds add some much-needed texture.

Serves 2

2 eggs
100ml whole milk
1 tablespoon Marmite, plus
   optional extra for drizzling
20g extra-mature cheddar, grated
2 slices of white bread
2 tablespoons white sesame
   seeds
a knob of unsalted butter

Crack the eggs into a wide, shallow bowl and whisk them together with the milk, Marmite and cheddar until combined. Dip both slices of bread into the eggy mixture, making sure both sides are well coated. Sprinkle the coated slices with the sesame seeds.

Melt the butter in a medium frying pan over a medium heat until it starts to froth. Add the slices of bread and cook, turning, until they are golden brown on both sides (it'll take about 3 minutes per side). Transfer the slices to a plate, cut them in half, drizzle them with extra Marmite (a must if you're truly a Lover) and enjoy!

Glazed meatballs with pickled cucumber

*Miso, honey and vinegar turn regular meatballs into sticky and sweet flavour bombs.
Here, I've paired them with pickled cucumber for some essential tanginess.*

Serves 1

2 teaspoons light miso
2 tablespoons runny honey
1 teaspoon malt vinegar
1 tablespoon pomegranate
  molasses
6 × 50/50 beef and pork
  meatballs
2 tablespoons vegetable oil
1 teaspoon white sesame seeds
salt and ground black pepper

For the pickled cucumber
1 cucumber, sliced into ribbons
1 red chilli, finely chopped
  (deseeded if you want less heat)
2 coriander sprigs, leaves picked
  and finely chopped
3 tablespoons malt vinegar

Mix together the miso, honey, malt vinegar and pomegranate molasses in a wide, shallow bowl with a pinch each of salt and pepper. Add the meatballs and turn them to coat them in the glaze.

Heat the oil in a medium frying pan over a medium heat. Add the glazed meatballs and cook, turning frequently, for about 8 minutes, until they are cooked through. You can spoon over any glaze that you have left in the bowl, if you like.

Meanwhile, make the pickled cucumber. Put the cucumber ribbons, chilli and coriander in a bowl, add the malt vinegar and leave the cucumber to marinate while the meatballs cook.

Remove the cooked meatballs from the pan and transfer them to a serving plate. Sprinkle them with the sesame seeds and serve them with the pickled cucumber.

Croque-madame flat bread

Creating the croque-madame experience on a flat bread, rather than in a toasted sandwich, makes the process a little easier, and I'm all for the pleasure of that! You'll need a firmer flat bread for this recipe – think a sturdy Greek option, rather than a Mexican tortilla.

Serve 2

40g unsalted butter
6 slices of smoked ham
1 teaspoon wholegrain mustard
1 garlic clove, crushed or grated
40g plain flour
150ml whole milk
100g gruyère, grated
1 large, sturdy flat bread
2 eggs
3 flat-leaf parsley sprigs, leaves
    picked and finely chopped

Melt the butter in a medium saucepan over a medium heat. Add the ham, mustard and garlic, cook for 1 minute to soften the garlic a little, then stir in the flour to make a paste. Cook for 1–2 minutes, to cook out the flour (this helps it to lose its floury flavour). Gradually add the milk to the paste, whisking continuously between each addition, until you have a thick, smooth sauce. Add the grated cheese and stir until melted.

Preheat the grill to high.

Place the flat bread on a baking sheet and spread the cheese and ham mixture over the top. Crack two eggs on top of the sauce and carefully transfer the baking sheet to the grill, cooking for 5–7 minutes, until the cheese is bubbling and the whites of the eggs are set (but the yolks are still runny).

Remove the baking tray from the grill, transfer the flat bread to a serving plate and sprinkle with parsley to serve.

Breaded pickles with truffle mayo

Pickles, breadcrumbs and mayo – a match made in culinary heaven. This American combination has been given the Life Kitchen makeover with truffle oil and parmesan boosting the umami flavours. It is total decadence.

Serves 2

1 egg
100ml whole milk
100g plain flour
100g Panko breadcrumbs
6 sweet-and sour-dill pickles,
  sliced into thick rounds
100ml vegetable oil, for frying

For the truffle mayo
½ tablespoon truffle oil
4 tablespoons mayonnaise
1 tablespoon English mustard

To serve
dried parmesan, for dusting
sea salt, for sprinkling

First, make the mayo by simply mixing together all the ingredients in a small bowl. Set it aside for later.

Combine the egg and milk in a small bowl. Tip the flour on to a small plate and the breadcrumbs on to another.

Take the pickles and dredge them first in the flour (shake off the excess), then in the egg mixture, and then in the breadcrumbs making sure they are coated on all sides. Set them on a baking tray ready for frying.

Heat the oil in a small frying pan over a medium heat. The oil is hot enough when you drop in a breadcrumb and it sizzles as soon as it hits the liquid.

Place a few pickles at a time into the hot oil and cook for 1 minute on each side, until the breadcrumbs are golden and crispy. Remove the cooked pickles from the pan and set them aside to drain on kitchen paper. Leave the oil to come back to temperature and repeat with the remaining pickles.

Transfer the cooked pickles to a serving dish, dust them with the dried parmesan and sprinkle them with a little sea salt, then serve with the truffle mayo for dipping.

White chocolate, cardamom and tahini strawberry pots

I'm a big fan of white chocolate. In this recipe, its sweetness is offset by the spicy cardamom and the nutty tahini. Add fruity strawberries and you've got the perfect bite in a pot.

Serves 4

8 frozen strawberries (or mango would work well, if you prefer), defrosted, plus optional extra to serve
200g white chocolate, broken into small pieces
150g unsalted butter, chopped into small pieces
3 cardamom pods, seeds removed and crushed
2 tablespoons tahini paste
400ml double cream
2 tablespoons crushed pistachios, to serve

Pop your strawberries into the bottom of 4 serving glasses or bowls (2 in each serving). Set aside.

Fill a large saucepan one-third full with freshly boiled water and place it over a medium heat. Put the chocolate and butter into a heatproof bowl and place the bowl on top of the pan of water (take care not to burn yourself – the pan will be steaming hot). Carefully stir together the butter and chocolate until they are melted and combined, then add the crushed cardamom seeds, the tahini and the double cream, stirring quickly to bring everything together.

Using a cloth to protect your hands, remove the bowl from the pan. Spoon the mixture equally between the serving pots to cover the strawberries, then leave the pots to cool. Once cooled, place them in the fridge for at least 2 hours to cool completely. Serve sprinkled with pistachios, and with a couple of extra strawberry halves on top, if you wish.

Pear and sweet soy caramel tarts

Sweet soy (also called kecap manis) is an unusual ingredient to find in a dessert, but its flavour adds a saltiness to the caramel that overall pairs beautifully with the fruity pears.

Serves 4

1 × 240g tin of pear halves,
  drained
4 shop-bought individual pastry
  cases
80g dark brown soft sugar
80g unsalted butter, cut into
  2cm cubes
½ teaspoon vanilla paste
250ml double cream
2 tablespoons kecap manis
  (sweet soy)
vanilla ice cream, to serve

Slice each pear half lengthways into three. Place the pastry cases on a baking tray.

In a large saucepan on a medium–low heat, add the soft brown sugar and the butter and stir, using a spatula to keep the sugar moving and make sure it doesn't catch on the sides of the pan and burn, until fully melted. Add in the vanilla paste, double cream and kecap manis, and whisk together to combine. The caramel needs to be thoroughly mixed. Bring the mixture to the simmer and cook for 1 minute, until thickened, then remove it from the heat.

Meanwhile, preheat the grill to medium.

Being careful as the caramel will be very hot, pour the caramel equally into each tart case so that it comes to 1cm below the rim. Place 3 pear slices into the centre of the caramel filling and push down slightly so that the pears sit in the sauce.

Place the tray of tarts under the grill for 1–2 minutes, until the pears are warmed and take on a little colour at the edges. Leave the tarts to cool slightly, then refrigerate to set for at least 2 hours. Serve with vanilla ice cream.

Cinnamon mascarpone apple turnovers

There's nothing new about an apple turnover, but, in my eyes, it is the definition of a perfect dessert. In this recipe, I've given that bite of sweet perfection a few simple twists – mascarpone, pomegranate molasses and lemon – turning it into something altogether better than even I thought it could be.

Serves 4

1 x 320g sheet of ready-rolled puff pastry
3 apples (Granny Smiths work best), peeled, cored and diced into 1cm cubes
100g caster sugar
¼ teaspoon ground cardamom
250g mascarpone
½ teaspoon ground cinnamon
1 egg, beaten
1 tablespoon demerara sugar

Preheat the oven to 180°C/160°C fan.

Trim the pastry sheet to make a square and cut the square into quarters, so that you have 4 equally sized square pieces of pastry. Place these in the fridge between pieces of baking paper (to stop them sticking together), leaving them chill while you make the apple.

Place the apple pieces into a small pan and add the caster sugar and cardamom. Place the pan on a medium heat and leave the apple to cook for 10 minutes, until it starts bubbling and is softened but not mushy. Remove the pan from the heat and leave the apple to cool for about 5 minutes.

Meanwhile, beat the mascarpone in a bowl with the cinnamon.

Remove the pastry squares from the fridge and spread 1 tablespoon of the spiced mascarpone mixture in to the middle of each, leaving a border around the edge. Then, spoon over equal amounts of the apple mixture.

Brush the edge of each pastry square with the beaten egg, then pick up one corner and fold it diagonally over the filling to meet the opposite corner, so that you end up with four filled pastry triangles. Press the open edges with the tines of a fork, to seal.

Space the triangles apart on a baking tray. Brush with some of the remaining beaten egg, to glaze, and sprinkle over the demerara sugar. Bake the turnovers in the oven for 20 minutes, until the filling is hot and the pastry is golden. Leave to cool for at least 10 minutes before picking up and tucking in, as the apple will be scalding.

Frozen yoghurt bombs (*tartufi*)

These little Italian flavour bombs are based on the miso white chocolate recipe from my first book, Life Kitchen. *I've replaced the double cream with yoghurt giving them a probiotic slant and encased them in pistachio for emerald decadence.*

Makes about 20

200g white chocolate, finely
   chopped or grated
100ml double cream
½ tablespoon white miso
100g full-fat extra-thick Greek
   yoghurt
1 tablespoon runny honey
200g shelled pistachios
10 cardamom pods, seeds
   removed (pods discarded)
edible rose petals (optional), torn

Place the chocolate in a heatproof bowl.

Heat the cream and miso paste together in a small saucepan over a medium heat, stirring to combine. When the mixture is almost boiling, remove the pan from the heat and pour the contents over chocolate. Stir until the chocolate is melted and the mixture is fully combined, then stir in the yoghurt and honey.

Place the bowl in the fridge, cover it and chill the mixture for at least 4 hours, but preferably overnight.

When you're ready to make the bombs, place the pistachios in a food processor with the cardamom seeds and blitz them to a crumb. Tip them into a shallow dish, with the rose petals, if using.

Remove the bowl of yoghurt mixture from the fridge. Using two teaspoons, one by one scoop balls of the chilled yoghurt and place them into the saucer of pistachio crumb, turning the balls to coat them entirely. Transfer each ball to a freezer-proof tray once coated. You should be able to make about 20 bombs in total.

Cover the tray loosely with cling film and transfer it to the freezer. Freeze the bombs for 1 hour, until firm, then transfer them to an airtight freezer container and store for up to 2 months. Leave each bomb at room temperature for 4–5 minutes before eating.

Apple and rose custard galette

A galette is a rustic-style French tart – a pastry case with a sweet or savoury filling and folded in around the edge. It is as simple as it is delicious. In this sweet version, the custard is laced with rose water to bring out the floral tones in the apple.

Serves 2-4

3 Pink Lady apples, halved, cored
  and thinly sliced
1 lemon, juiced
2 tablespoons demerara sugar,
  plus 2 teaspoons for the crust
250ml vanilla custard
zest of 1 orange
½ teaspoon rose water
1 × 320g sheet of ready-rolled
  shortcrust pastry
1 egg, lightly beaten with a dash
  of whole milk

Preheat the oven to 190°C/170°C fan.

Place the apple slices into a mixing bowl and add the lemon juice. Turn the apple to coat the slices in the juice, then sprinkle over the 2 tablespoons of sugar. Toss to distribute the sugar evenly.

In a separate, large mixing bowl, combine the vanilla custard, orange zest and rose water and mix well.

Lay out the pastry sheet on your work surface and use a dinner plate (about 18cm in diameter) to cut out a large circle from it. Transfer the pastry circle on to a lined baking tray. Discard the pastry trimmings.

Spoon 6 tablespoons of the custard mixture on to the pastry base, leaving a 2cm border around the edge. (Put the remaining custard in the fridge.) Carefully arrange the apples on top of the custard, starting at the outer edge and working inwards in concentric circles. Gently fold the edges of the pastry over the outermost ring of apple to form a rim. Brush the pastry edges with the egg mixture and sprinkle with the 2 teaspoons of sugar.

Bake the galette in the centre of the oven for 25 minutes, until the crust is golden and the apples are soft. Serve the tart warm with the chilled remaining custard.

Everything dessert sauce

Rose and orange blossom water form a fragrant and powerful base for this sauce, which does exactly what the title tells you – it is delicious drizzled over ice cream, tarts, cakes, meringues ... and more.

Serves 2

2 tablespoons rose water
2 tablespoons orange blossom
  water
2 tablespoons crushed pistachios
10 mint leaves, shredded
1 teaspoon vanilla paste

Mix all the ingredients together in a bowl until they are combined. Serve over any dessert you fancy for a powerful, indulgent kick.

Index

Cook's Notes

I've tested all the recipes in a regular fan oven, but have given both conventional and fan temperatures in the recipes. Remember, though, that ovens vary, so use the temperatures and timings as a guide and always check that your food is cooked through before eating.

Sterilise clean jars and lids by running them through the dishwasher on a hot cycle and leaving them to dry before removing. Or, 'bake' them in an oven at 200°C/180°C fan for 15 minutes.

Use fresh herbs and medium-sized eggs, vegetables and fruits unless the recipe states otherwise.

Always buy the best-quality ingredients you can afford, including organic meat, fish and produce whenever you can – but don't get hung up about this and remember to have fun with food! For the sake of our seas and rivers, though, please do buy fish (including tinned tuna) from sustainable sources.

Some recipes contain allergens – always check the packaging if you, or anyone you are cooking for, has food allergies or intolerances. Remember that, if you have low immunity, it's important to take care with ingredients such as raw or undercooked eggs. Consult your doctor if you are unsure as to the suitability of any ingredient or recipe.

Author's Thanks

This book would not have been possible without the help, commitment, advice and expertise of so many incredible people. You know who you are. Thank you.

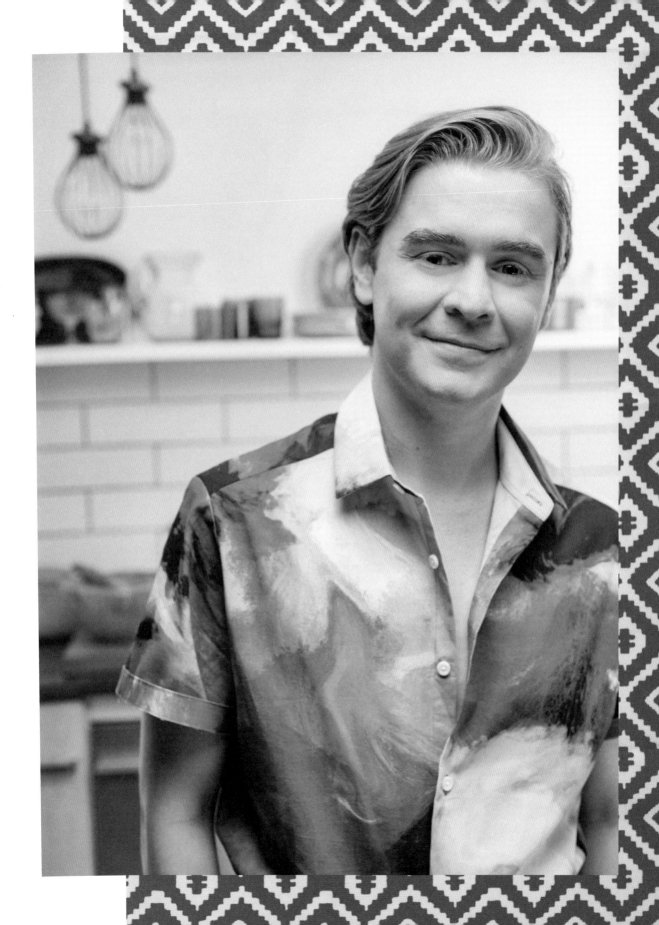

BLOOMSBURY PUBLISHING
Bloomsbury Publishing Plc
50 Bedford Square, London, WC1B 3DP, UK
29 Earlsfort Terrace, Dublin 2, Ireland

BLOOMSBURY, BLOOMSBURY PUBLISHING and the Diana logo are trademarks of Bloomsbury Publishing Plc

First published in Great Britain 2024

The information contained in this book is provided by way of general guidance in relation to the specific subject matters addressed herein, but it is not a substitute for specialist dietary advice. It should not be relied on for medical, healthcare, pharmaceutical or other professional advice on specific dietary or health needs. This book is sold with the understanding that the author and publisher are not engaged in rendering medical, health or any other kind of personal or professional services. The reader should consult a competent medical or health professional before adopting any of the suggestions in this book or drawing inferences from it.

The author and publisher specifically disclaim, as far as the law allows, any responsibility from any liability, loss or risk (personal or otherwise) which is incurred as a consequence, directly or indirectly, of the use and applications of any of the contents of this book.

A catalogue record for this book is available from the British Library

Library of Congress Cataloguing-in-Publication data has been applied for

Hardback 9781526626837
ePub 9781526626820
ePDF 9781526664846

2 4 6 8 10 9 7 5 3 1

Publisher: Rowan Yapp
Project Editors: Emily North and Judy Barratt
Designer: Anna Green, Siulen Design
Photographer: Craig Robertson
Food Stylist: Angela Boggiano
Prop Stylist: Kim Duke
Indexer: Hilary Bird

Printed by C&C Offset Printing Co. Ltd, China